Choosing Your Bigger Yes

5 Steps
to an
Authentically Happy Life

Volume One:
The Bigger Yes Series

Receive Your Life Publications
www.ReceiveYourLife.com

Choosing Your Bigger Yes

5 Steps
to an
Authentically Happy Life

Volume One:
The Bigger Yes Series

Janice Campbell

Receive Your Life®
Publications

CHOOSING YOUR BIGGER YES:
5 STEPS TO AN AUTHENTICALLY HAPPY LIFE

Published in the United States by Receive Your Life® Publications
www.receiveyourlife.com
Library of Congress Cataloging-in-Publication Data:
Campbell, Janice.
Choosing Your Bigger Yes / Janice Campbell.
1. Spirituality. 2. Self-Help. 3. Consciousness. 4. Self-Awareness.
5. Personal Growth. 6. Campbell, Janice.
Title:
CHOOSING YOUR BIGGER YES:
5 STEPS TO AN AUTHENTICALLY HAPPY LIFE
Library of Congress Control Number: (see website listed above)
ISBN-13: 978-0-9725063-2-8 (Paperback)
ISBN-13: 978-0-9725063-3-5 (Kindle eBook)
ISBN-13: 978-0-9725063-4-2 (Audio Book)
Note: Check website listed above for publication information on
Ebook and Audio Versions.
Published in the United States of America for US and worldwide distribution.
Receive Your Life® Publications
P.O. Box 631, San Anselmo, CA. 94979
Edited by Angela Browne-Miller.
Cover illustrations by Dennis Owens.
Author Photo by Jeanette Vonier.
Interior illustrations (maps, diagrams) and book layout by Angela Browne-Miller.
Ordering information and bulk ordering information available through:
Amazon Paperback and Amazon Kindle.
Also contact Info@ReceiveYourLife.com

To my husband, Hugh,
for his unwavering faith
in this work and in me.

Table of Contents

A Note About Your Bigger Yes

You may be wondering what your bigger yes is. Best to ask *who* this bigger yes is, because this bigger yes is the real you.

Choosing your bigger yes is making choices that align with your authentic self. Your bigger yes is the unique expression of the life that you came here to live, and of the self you came here to evolve.

The world wants the true you, not the false you. And you want this too. It is time to come out and truly live, truly and authentically participate in life, in *your* life. You are perfectly designed to make the contribution you came here to make and to share the gift that you are. It is time to say yes to you and to the life that wants to be lived through you and as you.

No one is going to come along and grant you permission to be your authentic self. This is an inside job. We've all heard the saying, "Say yes to life." Well, the real YES TO LIFE happens once you say YES TO YOURSELF, once you truly appreciate who you really are.

Your bigger yes
is the
celebration of you.

This is saying yes to
who you really are.

Say yes to living your life as openly and honestly as you can. It is time to be yourself. No more hiding who you are. No more pretending you are someone you are not.

Living a watered down version of who you are doesn't work for you. And it doesn't work for the people around you, nor does it work for the planet.

Once we wake up to this understanding, we stop withholding ourselves, we stop questioning whether what we have to share actually has value. Our inner conflicts and confusions then dissolve.

Being you is far easier than not being you. Being *authentic* is the word I like best to describe it: living the authentic version of you, reclaiming who you truly are:

CHOOSING YOUR BIGGER YES!

Author's Note

I myself know how important it is to live as one's authentic self, to reclaim and further evolve that self. I spent years trying to find a way through my questions about my life and the challenges in my life. In hindsight I realize that what I was really searching for was my way home, back to my own authentic self.

The 5 Steps I share in this book are the core of the Receive Your Life System I have developed over the years. These 5 Steps did not come to me as an instant download. I worked with all this moment by moment over a period of years: coaching clients, teaching, studying, walking, writing, talking with my husband, meditating, hoping to gain greater clarity both for myself and for others. This Receive Your Life System I have developed includes 5 Steps, 5 Basic Step Exercises, and several other exercises and practices. The first books in this Bigger Yes Series present basic processes applying these 5 Steps and their exercises and practices. This first volume explains the process of Choosing Your Bigger Yes.

My own story helped bring me to the understandings I share in this book. Earlier in my career, I spent years as a Certified Public Accountant and Financial Planner. There were parts of that work I enjoyed and parts I definitely did not enjoy or find rewarding. The part I loved the most was having conversations with people about their money and how that connected to what mattered most to them. Since then, over the last twenty plus years, I have been studying spiritual principles and coaching people in applying those principles to their everyday lives. Helping people explore why we do what we do, why we want what we want, and why we struggle in life, has been a never ending source of fascination and satisfaction for me.

The *5 Steps* offered in this book are a culmination of my studies and observations. I am writing this book for a very specific reason. In my many years of coaching, there is a pattern I've noticed. People have huge misunderstandings about who they are and the value they bring to the world and to themselves. Yet many people do not reveal these misunderstandings to themselves let alone to the world. So much of what I am talking about here is not readily visible. People tend not to show all their anxieties on the surface level.

In fact, many people I see in my work appear to be walking around very proud and confident of who they are. Yet underneath there is something else going on. They are struggling on some level. Many people are struggling with their perceived inadequacies and are unaware of the power and pure goodness that they truly are. I know from my years of coaching people, working quite closely with them, that the essence that lies deep inside all of us is beautiful and magnificent.

Regardless of the value we place on outer appearances, we actually do live from the inside out. We do this even though we may be unaware that this is what we are doing. If we are experiencing peace and wholeness within ourselves, that is what we will experience in the world. If we are battling our inner conflicts, what we will experience is a world of conflict. You don't have to agree or disagree with me right now, you can experience this for yourself as you read and work through the exercises in this book.

Your experience of the world you live in and your ability to impact it in a positive way will shift as you work through the 5 Steps I share here. You will very clearly be able to discern the difference between your true self and your false self. I absolutely know this to be possible.

I have compiled these steps for you so you don't have to take as long as I did to become aware of your authentic self. You see, living authentically has very little to do with time. This is not about how much time you have put into getting to this place right here right now, this place where you are ready to learn to choose your ***bigger yes***. You are here, right here, reading this book and can put these steps to work in your life at any time you choose. And these steps will take you right to your authentic self.

Yes, ***you can most definitely break through*** to your authentic self. This is not hard, as your authentic self is already here right now. Just keep in mind that you deserve to have the breakthroughs you desire. These 5 Steps will support you on this ***journey to you***. What I have learned from working with this Receive Your Life System and its Choosing Your Bigger Yes Process is that every time you get a glimpse of your value and the gift that you are your world expands. You receive a wonderful infusion of energy and your life feels so much better. The deeper your realization and appreciation of your true self, the more satisfying your experience of life, of all life, becomes.

Choosing Your Bigger Yes is simple. What this requires is (1) an awareness that you do have a true self, and (2) an understanding of what your true self is about. This book guides you in this process of reclaiming your self and your life through awareness and understanding.

The journey to your truest, most authentic, life is your very own hero's journey. When you are on this journey to your true self, to your authentic self, you are on a very personal journey. Yet when on this, your own personal journey, you are demonstrating to all of us what we are all about. Enjoy the journey. It will be like no other you have been on.

Janice Campbell
Marin County, California

PART ONE

1
Knowing and Reclaiming True Happiness

Happiness, happiness, happiness.

We want happiness. We talk about being happy, wanting to be happy, wanting to find happiness. All around us, everywhere we look, we see the signs of happiness and unhappiness. Yet if we ask ourselves, we do not really know what true happiness is about, what it is made of, where it comes from, how to get it. Not really.

We are more engaged with the superficial definitions of happiness we hear coming at us than with the deep happiness we are entirely able to achieve. We have to ask why.

There is definitely more to learn about this thing we call happiness and the experience of satisfaction that is part of it. We are designed to be happy. Yet if we are designed to experience the true happiness available to us, what is it that so often keeps us from doing so?

This book, *Choosing Your Bigger Yes,* is about finding true happiness by discovering and being who you truly are. This is about evolving more and more of yourself each day. This is the process of your own personal evolution where you know and reclaim the authentic satisfaction deep within you.

This book takes you through the process of choosing your bigger yes. You can say YES to your true self. You CAN reclaim your true self. You can evolve yourself in your own way at your own speed. Here you will read about what it means to …

Make the choice to choose your bigger yes each step of the way.

You deserve to live the rich and satisfying life you have been given to live. By working with the *5 Steps* contained on these pages, you will recognize the gift that you are. You will see that these are indeed *5 Steps to an Authentically Happy Life.* This book will provide you with tools to consciously choose true deep happiness and the true satisfaction that comes with this choice.

These *5 Steps to An Authentically Happy Life* are not simply the same old general tips, the ones that we've all heard before: wonderful notions such as kindness, gratitude, forgiveness, service, love, loyalty, etc. This book goes beyond the platitudes and provides insights and exercises that will help you access the unique happiness that lives deep within you.

These 5 Steps have been inspired by the many people I have had, and continue to have, the pleasure of working with through the years. Many of their journeys begin with a longing, a yearning, a divine discontent. Many of them feel on some level called to a fuller expression of themselves and their lives.

These are people who, just like most of us, wake up to the realization that there is more to life than what they are living. Some of the conversations start like these:

> "Nothing ever seems to work out for me. Things go well for a while but then they always fall apart. I keep trying to go after what I want but I just can't seem to get there."

> "I never feel I am being myself. I don't know what that means, but I still have this nagging feeling that I have no idea where I am going or why. Earlier in my life, I thought I would eventually figure this out. But now, after years have gone by and I don't know any more than I did when I was younger, I am wondering if this is all life has to offer me."

> "It seems like almost everyone else is more satisfied than I am. I keep getting the feeling that I am off track and that I will never find the right road."

> "I keep feeling like a failure even though everyone tells me I am successful."

Every week clients tell me they are feeling confused, lost, trapped, stuck. They tell me they want to understand more about their lives and their choices, about themselves. Many talk to me about life situations such as these:

> "I had a business with my wife. After eighteen years of marriage, my wife left me saying that she just didn't want to do it anymore. We finally got our divorce six years ago. I haven't been able to get back on my feet with work and making money. How am I supposed to feel? What am I supposed to be doing? How am I supposed to make money? Other people say try this or try that, but none of it makes much sense. I'm drifting and feeling lost. I don't know who I am anymore."

> "I work on my job fourteen to sixteen hours a day. At home, I have a horse, other animals, and a garden. These are nice to have, but I do not have much free time to do what I want to do. I am getting very angry and resentful about what my job is doing to my life. I take it out on everything. I even yell at my computer. I know my anger is affecting my health. And all this work I am doing does not even cover my bills. I'm working on commission and don't make much. But I am concerned about stopping work. Then what?"

> "I feel lost and stuck in my marriage. I don't know if this is my fault or his, or no one's. I just don't feel like being close to my husband. Every time I start to trust him and open up about my feelings, he blows up and gets irrational. I don't want to keep repeating this cycle I've been repeating for years, throughout my marriage. We even divorced at one point and then got back together for the kids. I realize now that part of the reason I am staying with him is because of the finances, although even this part of our lives is stressful. We are an emotional mess on a daily basis. This doesn't work for me. So, recently I have been trying not to be too stressed and upset, to just let go of caring, to just not pay attention to all this. To do this, I make myself seem preoccupied and

disconnected. This works for me some, and at times I do feel a little better. But now my husband has a very sad look on his face most of the time and is getting more and more depressed. I do not know what to think."

Have you ever asked yourself questions like these: "Why am I not happy? Why can't I get what I want? Why doesn't my life look the way I want it to look?" Many people look at their situations and feel that their lives are totally out of their control. But is there another way to see things and is there another way to experience life? Yes there is.

There is a beautiful mystery to life, one that we will never fully comprehend. There is so much about ourselves and our situations and the whole of our lives that we cannot fully see at any one time. And yet there is so much we can be doing for ourselves, so much we can do with so little effort, so much that will yield huge dividends in the quality of our lives.

Many of us have learned to go through life on automatic pilot. We may not know why we do what we do, or why we feel what we feel, we just do whatever we do automatically. We just get by, another day, another dollar. If our alarm clock goes off at 6 a.m. each morning, we're not surprised when 6 a.m. rolls around and the alarm goes off. We wake up and today is pretty much like yesterday. Sure there may be a few highlights, special events along the way, but we pretty much know how our life is going to look in the next 10, 20 or 40 years.

Now that would be a perfectly fine life were it not for those desires and longings that keep creeping in, those subtle feelings of wanting more or different. Yes, that would be a perfectly fine life were it not for that divine discontent coming over you from time to time, welling up from deep inside you. What are you supposed to do with these feelings? Ignore them? Hope they will go away? Talk yourself out of wanting what you want?

You may be able to do this for awhile, but at some point resisting who you are and what you want starts to wear you down; lethargy, despair and hopelessness become your familiar companions. Fortunately there is a way to bring yourself back to your natural state of happiness and fulfillment.

The natural state of true happiness and fulfillment begins *with knowing the truth of who you are.* This knowing begins with having an understanding of how your energy naturally flows. Once you can sense this flow of your energy, you can consciously align your thoughts, words and actions with the flow of this energy.

This is the journey of
Choosing Your Bigger Yes,
the path to
your authentic self.

You can choose this journey. You can choose your own bigger yes. You can move from feeling unfulfilled and powerless in life to knowing you can carve out your own reality.

2
Happy is More Than A Five Letter Word

Let's talk about happiness again here because understanding what true happiness is helps us reclaim the happiness that is ours to have.

Everywhere we turn, we hear the world sending us messages about what will make us happy: buy this, do that, listen to this, be part of that – all to be happy. And many of us are driven to pursue this sort of happiness, what the world tells us is happiness.

Yet all of this talk about happiness may not be reaching the real deep and very personal place of fulfillment, the actual happiness possible for each and every one of us.

You see, happiness is far more than something we can "get" when we listen to commercials, people on television, leaders of clubs and movements, friends, family, and so on.

Too often, we are quite confused about what it means to be happy. Yet true happiness is ours, we already carry this deep within ourselves. True happiness is all about a very personal sense of fulfillment and deep connection with oneself when making one's choices and decisions in life.

True happiness comes from deep inside yourself and is not defined by the outside world.

3
Going for Authentic Happiness

Authentic happiness is about being real with yourself, being honest with yourself about what it is that makes you authentically happy. I say "authentically" happy here because this is about being authentic with yourself. Authentic happiness is about being real, being your true self, expressing who you really are, being deeply fulfilled by your choices because your choices are *your own choices* and they reflect what you value.

Authentic happiness is a deep sense of fulfillment, not just a surface or superficial happiness. While happiness is almost always a welcome feeling, much happiness is surface happiness, meaning that if you dig just a little deeper, that surface happiness is only that: on the surface. It is fleeting and without roots. Authentic happiness is richer than surface happiness.

Surface happiness is about trying to control our circumstances. We are convinced that once we get the world to line up perfectly, then we will be happy. Again and again, we find that this surface happiness involves the belief that our happiness is dependent upon people and situations outside of ourselves.

Have you ever heard yourself criticize others' behaviors, convinced that if only they would behave differently or do what you want them to do, then you would be happy – as if they have the power to withhold your happiness from you? Or have you ever told yourself that if only you had more money, lived in a different location, had a different spouse, job, kids, etc., then you would be happy?

You may hear yourself saying something like this: "I'm not like all those other people who have gotten all the goodies they want and are still unhappy. I'm different. Just watch, bring me everything I want and I promise I will be happy." It is easy to say this to ourselves, because it is easy to believe this is true. You see, *we've been taught for so long that happiness flows from the outside in.*

Approaching happiness from this outside-in direction has us harboring a lot of anger and resentment. We feel powerless and frustrated that we can't have what we want. We tell ourselves that "once everything is in place and people are doing what they are supposed to be doing, then I will be happy." We can spend a lifetime waiting for this superficial version of happiness. And not only will we be waiting a long time, we will be chasing an illusion. And chasing this illusion of happiness is exhausting.

If you have found yourself engaged in this type of conversation with yourself, this is an indication that you have been chasing surface happiness. This is both good and bad news. The bad news is that this chasing after something that does not have the capacity to deliver true happiness gets old.

Yet the good news is that your desire for happiness is alive and well. Deep within, deep down inside, you know happiness is your natural state. You can understand the conundrum you find yourself in. You don't want to give up on your dream of happiness because in your heart and soul you know you deserve to be happy. Still, somehow, happiness can continue to feel just one step beyond where you are. You can hear yourself swimming in the "if only….." conversations. Yet authentic happiness is already here, within you. This has nothing to do with the outside world.

I'm not saying that beautiful homes, loving relationships, satisfying careers are not worth having. They most definitely are. And when you approach happiness from the inside out, you will be able to experience both the deep inner and the more surface outer happiness simultaneously. You will also see the difference between these.

Know that authentic happiness is entirely possible and is deeply satisfying. It is your birthright.

Authentic happiness originates from within your soul and grows outward.

When you bring your awareness to your inner knowing and act on what you know to be true, an authentic happiness can blossom both within and around you. True happiness is an effect. It is the byproduct of living as your authentic self. Authentic happiness involves knowing yourself well enough to see whether the choices you are making are either supporting or sabotaging you.

It is important to recognize the difference. This is the key to being truly happy, to making authentically gratifying choices. But first you must know yourself.

So authentic happiness involves you living by your values, living by your internal knowing. Your inner wisdom guides you in the direction of being who you really are, of living an inspired life: your life. The following of this inspiration is moment by moment. This involves making moment to moment choices and decisions on the path to inner satisfaction and fulfillment.

Authentic happiness is about allowing yourself to truly know yourself. Through the processes offered in this book, you will have the tools to see the difference, to know when you are searching for surface happiness and when you are embracing your authentic happiness. These two paths do feel quite different.

With a little practice, you will see this difference every time you make a choice or decision in life. You will be ever more clear about which path you are following. One path has you chasing your "shoulds" and attempting to experience surface happiness from the outside in. And the other path has you acting on your inner knowing.

Many people live inside the lie of surface happiness. This lie says that if you follow all the "shoulds" you hear, you will be rewarded with a prize at the end. This message is a setup. You see, that reward never really arrives. And the reason it never really arrives is because that reward is not about your real self or life. That surface reward is based on someone else's opinion of what your life "should" be and yet to you it is a compromise.

The truth is that you don't really want what is on the other end of those shoulds coming at you from the outside world. You want your own authentic self and life. You want to reclaim and live your true self and life, not the self and life you are told you should want to be and live.

Now of course, there are many times when we do listen to others' opinions because we see value in what they are sharing. There is nothing wrong with doing this. However, it is best to run what we hear coming at us through our inner knowing filters. We can feel our deepest responses to messages that come at us from the outside world and we can then make authentic choices and decisions about these.

In other words, we do not simply let the outside world direct and guide us in life. We want to let our inner selves direct and guide us.

True, authentic, happiness is not derived from following a list of shoulds coming at us from outside ourselves. True happiness comes from deep inside. Authentic happiness is what you experience by aligning with your own energy.

Authentic happiness is the natural expression of living as your true self. Your capacity for the joy of expressing who you truly are, of being your authentic self, is unlimited.

4
Deep Satisfaction and the Authentic Self

Deep satisfaction is the result of living as your authentic self. And as important as satisfaction is to us, its actual meaning often does not get enough attention. Now, most of us have experienced some degree of satisfaction at times. Perhaps we did a job well, baked a great cake, or walked two miles every day last week.

We do know the experience of satisfaction. However, do we know the deepest form of satisfaction? Do we know the difference between deep satisfaction experienced on the soul level, and other more surface level satisfaction? Surface level satisfaction is often confused with deep satisfaction.

Surface level satisfaction is shallow, fleeting or short lived, and it is not entirely satisfying. It is that feeling we have when we think we should be satisfied, when we tell ourselves we *should* be satisfied, while deep within we hear ourselves saying, "I am not feeling satisfied." Do you ever criticize yourself for not being entirely satisfied, wondering why you are not satisfied when any normal person would be satisfied with your situation?

Deep satisfaction is
what you experience
when you harmonize
with
yourself, your spirit, your soul.

When your thoughts, your words, and your actions align with your authentic self, you feel it. There is a peace that washes over you. And you know you are in harmony with your authentic self.

Achieving this harmony with your authentic self involves sorting out any inner conflicts you may have about being authentic with yourself. And this involves deciding to focus your consciousness on your true self.

Deep satisfaction is what you experience when you say yes to who you really are, rather then yes to who you believe you should be. Your authentic self most definitely wants to live the fullest expression of who you are and does not want to hold itself – the true you – back.

When you realize it is safe to be who you are, you release yourself from the fear and hesitation of your limited self. You then feel powerful in your life and know you are able to create what you desire, that what you truly want is within your reach. You gain a traction that you did not have access to when living as your limited self.

Breathe deeply into this knowing that when you are being your authentic self you are living in integrity with yourself:

You are not selling out.
You are not compromising.
You are not pretending to be something other than who you truly are.

You can have this knowing that you are on track with your life and that everything will unfold in the perfect time. You can release the stress of believing you are not enough or not doing enough. You can relax into knowing that you are enough and that there is nothing missing within you.

Through the steps in this book you will have the experience of living from the feeling of having enough – enough time, enough energy, enough creativity – enough to do what your heart desires to do. Enough is not an amount of money or minutes. Enough is a state of mind. You will be able to express your authentic self and experience deep satisfaction. You will be at peace with yourself and your choices.

5
The Meaning of Your Life

Does your life have meaning? If so, what is that meaning? Who decides what the meaning of your life is? Do you decide this? Is the answer the same for everyone? Do some people decide for themselves what the meaning of their lives are, while others have people around them telling them what the meaning of their lives should be?

Bottom line, the meaning of your life is what is most important about your life. And the meaning of your life is up to you to define. What your life is about is ...

what your life is about
in your own eyes and heart.

If you at times find yourself wondering whether your life has meaning, this is a good thing. This means you are asking yourself a question that can take you back to yourself. You are looking for meaning that is already there within you. You can reclaim this meaning of your life, as this belongs to you, as this is already there deep within you.

This meaning is you. This understanding will not look the same for each person. What is meaningful for one person is not necessarily meaningful for another.

Seeing the meaning of one's life is a journey each one of us has to go on. Each person's journey is a very personal one, very specific to each person. So ask yourself: what is the meaning of my life? What has meaning for me? What am I perfectly designed to know, to see and to be?

Many people turn away from knowing these things for one reason or another. Quite often we let the outside world tell us what we know and see, and what to do. We do this even when we feel pulled in a different direction from deep inside, pulled to listen to ourselves for the truth of who we are.

Think about the course of your life and the course of your feelings about your life. When did you feel you were being honest with yourself about who you are? What about the times you sensed on some level that you were not being entirely true to yourself, not being your authentic self. When you turn away from the truth of who you are, you are turning away from the meaning of your life.

When you turn away from the truth of who you are, you may be believing that you have to be somebody else, somebody other than who you really are. You can feel this turning away from yourself if you pay close attention to yourself.

You may feel as if you are going through the motions of being alive, but not being fully alive. You may feel as if you are going through the motions of being yourself, but not being fully yourself, not being your authentic self. You may be aware that something is missing.

Each of us is perfectly designed, perfectly designed to attune to ourselves and our purpose. And when we are not fully aligned with our purpose, when we are not really living the fullest expression of who we really are, we can feel it. We can feel that something is not quite right. For example, we may hear things like this: you should be grateful, you should be this, you should be that.

When we hear things like this, we try to do what we hear we should do and feel. We try to pump ourselves up, but there is still something that feels off. We may be successful by worldly standards, or we may be struggling to get by. Yet we can feel something is not quite right either way. At this point we have to take ourselves, our true selves, seriously.

We have to matter to ourselves.
We have to know what matters.

What does matter is how you feel in your heart and soul. Do you feel connected to what you are doing? Does what you are doing infuse you with life and joy and peace? It doesn't matter exactly what you are doing. What matters is the feeling of being connected to yourself. When you are truly connected to yourself, there are so many things you can be doing that will bring you joy and satisfaction.

Being connected to yourself starts at your core, with connecting on a deep level to yourself. This connecting with yourself will be so very very personal to you. You are the only one who can answer this question:

Am I living
a meaningful life?

It's not up to the world to judge whether or not your own life is meaningful to you. Each one of us is measuring meaning in a very personal way. We measure for something very specific to ourselves. And yet choosing our own bigger yes, choosing to be our own authentic self, benefits everyone.

At first it may appear to you, or maybe to some of those around you, that all this talk about having a meaningful life is quite self-centered, even somewhat selfish. However, being your authentic self is not a bad thing for you or for those around you.

Being more of your true self is sharing the gift that you are. It is the highest and best of what you have to offer both yourself and the world you share with others.

**This is a self-centered approach
in a good way.**

**You are taking responsibility
for your happiness
rather than expecting
the world
to provide it for you.**

6
The Part You Play in the Unfolding of the Universe

If you are alive, you are a part of the unfolding of the Universe. Do you know what your part is? Are you aware of your place in the Universe – of the meaning of your life?

As you are moving toward expressing and living as your authentic self, saying YES TO YOURSELF, you may ask yourself: Is it fair that I get to live a meaningful life when other people can't? Please just let this question dissolve because:

Each of us can live
a meaningful life.

Each of us is
perfectly designed to
live the life
we have been given to live.

Take this knowledge in. You can, you DO, have a meaningful life. The goal here is to help you reclaim your sense of having a meaningful life.

Certainly there are things that get in the way of our seeing this, feeling this about our lives. However, we CAN move past these blocks to ourselves, to our lives. We can reclaim ourselves and our lives.

This has nothing to do with material things such as money, cars, houses, clothes. However, we often use not having "enough" money and/or other material things as an excuse to not see or not be our authentic selves. We may tell ourselves that if we do not have enough things or money, we are not able to be who we are or are not quite ready to share the gift that we are.

When we use money or anything outside ourselves (money, cars, clothes, or even less material things outside ourselves such as relationships, accomplishments, opportunities) as an excuse for not being who we are, we limit the flow of energy to and from ourselves. We constrict our giving and receiving flow.

And then we can grow resigned, or maybe even depressed, resentful, or bitter. We can find ourselves expressing very little of the essence of who we are. We may feel our energy constricting. We can find ourselves separating away from ourselves. And yet, the way back to ourselves is not far. We are not far from ourselves. In fact, we are already there. We are already who we are: our authentic selves. We just need to reclaim ourselves for ourselves. We owe this to ourselves.

**You just have to know
that
it is safe to be
your authentic self.**

When we connect with our true selves, with what is meaningful to our authentic selves – our truest values, gifts and desires – then we are at home with ourselves. Then we are finding our authentic selves and saying yes to our authentic selves.

This may all sound a bit overwhelming at this point but rest assured there is nothing missing within you. Your authentic self is already whole, complete and perfect, waiting to be discovered by you. The steps and exercises in this book will gently guide you back home to your true self.

PART TWO

7
Are You Living an Authentic Life?

Living an authentic life is not just some dream, some kind of unachievable ideal. The authentic self you already carry within you is already right here, ready to be expressed in the form of your authentic life.

**We all carry within us
our very own
authentic selves.**

**Just let
your authentic self
live
your authentic life.**

**Just be
who you really are.**

Sounds simple? Is it? Yes, once you understand what this means. Let's talk about the authentic self who lives the authentic life. First of all, if you are not living as your authentic self, then who are you living as? Whose life have you defaulted to? Could this life you are living be the life you have been told to live by your parents, your teachers, your spouse, your community, or maybe even your culture?

Could you have gotten here, living this particular expression of life, without realizing this is not who you are? Have you found yourself wondering what is going on, what you are really feeling?

After years of trying to do the "right thing" and being obedient to everyone else's agenda except your own, have you ever considered the possibility that you are here to live life in a way that reflects your true nature?

You may find yourself living your life, being who you are and doing what you do, based on what the world around you says you should be and do. It is easy to drift into the habit of living from the outside in. It is easy to look to your circumstances and your environment to tell you who you should be and what you should want. (And over time you may find yourself actually believing all those shoulds.) Most of us have been in this situation. Many of us still are.

Over time, living this way causes us to lose touch with our authentic selves. We grow confused, we start to doubt ourselves, and we end up living a fraction of the life we came here to live.

Too often, we fall into the trap of believing we have to be someone other than who we are to attain the satisfaction we desire. If this belief continues for too long, the uneasy feeling of selling out creeps in. We then can feel out of integrity with ourselves, in conflict with ourselves, even though we cannot say exactly why.

This deep, often unexplainable inner conflict becomes the source of a very uncomfortable unhappiness. We feel we have sold out, yet we are not clear what this means to us. We sell out or compromise by being someone other than who we truly are when this inauthentic life appears to be our only option.

If you are feeling less than enthusiastic about being alive, chances are you are living a diluted version of who you came here to be. The life you were born to live is waiting to be embraced by you.

The satisfaction and peace of living a life that is meaningful to you is awaiting your receptivity.

Simply by choosing your bigger yes, you can reclaim your life.

As you read on in this book, you will see how *Choosing Your Bigger Yes* is a step by step process, a roadmap taking you to yourself, your authentic self. The material in this book can guide you to the richness of your life. Know that the further you travel into knowing your true self, the more inspired you will become by your life.

As you strengthen your understanding of your true self, you will be able to reduce your reliance on outside authorities – gurus, teachers, ministers, authors, parents, therapists, coaches. Of course these people can support you on the path to living as your authentic self, yet they cannot tell you who you truly are. Only you know who you truly are.

Instead of looking to others first for answers about yourself and your life, begin your journey by looking within. The only expert on your life is you. No one else has access to what lives within your heart and soul. The *5 Steps* described later in this book will help you discover who you are and who you are not. You will be able to solve problems such as: "Why do I feel my life doesn't work?" and "How can I get my life to work?"

As you move forward here, just keep in mind that your life can work quite well. Your life may simply be buried under an avalanche of "shoulds" coming at you from outside yourself. Always remember that who you are hasn't gone anywhere. Who you are is right here waiting to come out and play.

The following pages will help you release beliefs and expectations that do not belong to you. You can do this, you can stand firm as your full and powerful self, fully knowing and expressing the love, beauty and wholeness that you are.

8
What Being Happy and Unhappy Is All About

Although we can see that there is a great deal of happiness in the world, we can also find signs of people's unhappiness. For example, we see people using antidepressants, alcohol or other drugs to fight depression and loneliness, shame, and even suicidal thinking. These people often find themselves trapped in addictions they cannot get away from. We also see road rage, work arguments, families fighting, and shootings. We see broken relationships and marriages and the pain and confusion these bring. All of this unhappiness is telling us something.

Both unhappiness and happiness are important pieces of information. Our levels of happiness and unhappiness are indicators of how we are feeling and of how we are moving, flowing, our energy.

In other words, feeling happy and/or unhappy tells us a lot about *how* we are doing, and tells us *how we feel* about what we are doing, and tells *us how well our energy is moving* in all of this.

Do we feel we have a say in how our energy moves and feels to us? Do we have dominion over our own energy? Or does something or someone beside ourselves decide how our energy flows?

Do we choose how we use our energy? Or are we just reacting to how life comes at us, just letting the outside world determine whether we are happy about how we are using our energy?

If we are living life based on what the outside world tells us to do and feel, we are living life from the outside in. We are looking out into the world to determine our level of happiness. When things seem to be going well, lining up with what we want, we feel happy, our energy flows freely and we feel good. This works for us as long as everything outside ourselves lines up with what we truly want.

However, this does not always happen for us. There are many things that are outside our control. For example, if we have children and they are behaving in a way that we approve of, we are happy.

But when they are behaving in a way that we don't approve of, we become unhappy. We are reacting to the way our children are behaving, and in doing this, we are living from the outside in – we are reacting to our circumstances.

We feel powerless because we cannot control things around us. And of course, no one can control all of life's circumstances. Still, many of us use our energy trying to change and even fix the outside world. We keep telling ourselves that, "If I can just get everything to line up perfectly, then I will be happy."

If we are searching for happiness from the outside in, we are constantly disappointed with people and life. "If only they would … then I would be happy." This is a powerless way to go through life.

You can tell when you are searching for happiness based on what is coming at you from outside yourself – you can tell this by how you feel. Some common feelings that can tell you are: disappointment, resentment, anger, bitterness, impatience, frustration, depression, confusion, exhaustion, etc. You are waiting, always waiting for the circumstances you are in to change. It feels like your life is on hold.

This state of mind can be tricky because very often it feels like what we want is so close. We're almost there. "If I just could make a little more money, have a little more time." "If I just tried a little harder, got a little better." "If my politician just gets elected, the tax laws will change, then I will be happy."

But true happiness doesn't work that way. What a set-up it is, this thinking happiness is something we can chase and catch.

Our happiness is unique to us. And what allows one person to experience happiness may not do it for another. We each have our own path to happiness. And that path is to be comfortable in our own skin, to live in integrity with ourselves.

What this means is that there is an authentic you, a real, true, honest you. When you align your thoughts, words and actions with your true self, you are happy. When you are experiencing inner conflicts in trying to pretend you are someone you are not, or in working to fit in and gain the approval of others, you are compromising and you won't be truly, authentically, happy.

When you choose to live
purposely, authentically,
truly in the
flow of your own life,
you will feel the
true happiness that you are.

9
The Value of Dissatisfaction

The word "happiness" is tricky because it means so many different things to people. I am happy or I am not happy are states of mind that change like the wind. Very often, our relationship to happiness has to do with our circumstances. As discussed in the previous chapter, too often we feel our relationship to happiness is removed from us and instead is defined by the world around us. Being unhappy is therefore not as simple as it sounds.

Dissatisfaction is even more complicated than unhappiness. The feelings of satisfaction and dissatisfaction are deep. These feelings connect people to their souls. When we long for satisfaction, we want something deeper than simple happiness. There is a knowing deep within us that we desire to, long to, connect with.

Desiring this knowing is wanting to come home to your true self, to be one with yourself, with Spirit, God, or the Universe, depending on how you choose to label this. Seeking this connection is the longing that lives within each one of us. Even if we may be ignoring the presence of this spirit, this flow of life, it is always calling out for us to reunite with it.

When we turn toward Spirit, toward our connection with God or with the Universe, with the flow of life, we feel peace, love and contentment. We then feel a rightness about our lives. We are connecting with our true selves which in turn connect us with all of life.

When we are turning away from our truest selves, we feel dissatisfaction. You may have felt this dissatisfaction. It is that feeling you have when you can't really explain why something doesn't feel right, it just doesn't feel right.

Dissatisfaction is about a disconnection within us. Often this shows up as a feeling of loneliness or separateness.

Most of us have experienced dissatisfaction. We know the feeling that something is off while not quite knowing what to do about it. We know what it is like to experience an inner conflict, one where our energy is trying to go in two different directions. We know what it feels like to not know which direction to move in, to not know where to line up our energy.

You may realize that there have been times you were aligning with your false, compromised, inauthentic self. You see,

dissatisfaction
is being out of harmony with
your authentic self.

When your energy is stuck and not flowing, there is a backlog of frustrated energy that doesn't know where to go so it keeps running in circles. You are trying, trying, trying, but just can't get to where you want to go. When this is going on, you know on some level that there is more to your life.

You may know on some level that there is more to your life than what you are experiencing. But you may feel powerless to go after it.

There is a wisdom within us that knows this feeling can't be bridged through circumstances: the outside world cannot solve this problem. We probably have tried to let the outside world solve such a problem and found that this hasn't yielded the results we wanted. This is because we have misunderstood what dissatisfaction is really about.

If we are looking out into the world, listening to the various opinions about how we should be and feel, and comparing ourselves with how others seem to be and feel, we can feel separate from our true selves. When you are separate from your true self, you may feel pain. If there is pain being felt, then know that the pain in life comes from not fully understanding the gift that you are and the value you have to share. Know that there is wisdom in your dissatisfaction because it is alerting you that something is off.

You may be listening to something other than the truth of who you are. And when you listen to a lie, this doesn't feel good. And to feel better, you may run around chasing what you believe will ease the pain. But feeling better, truly better, just doesn't work this way. You can only be healed, have a realization of your wholeness, from the inside out. Mother Teresa once said that many people today are spiritually starved. We are spiritually starved when we look to be filled up in ways that are incapable of satisfying us.

The good news is that we don't need outside resources to fill us up. The feeling of satisfaction and fulfillment is something we can give to ourselves. This feeling is already within us. It is saying yes to who we came here to be. It is turning away from who we have been told by the outside world that we should be. It is turning to ourselves, turning to be the person we truly are.

This is not about material riches. Being surrounded by the riches of the world cannot bring us the deep sense of fulfillment we desire. That desire within us is the light that leads us back to our true selves.

10
Life IS Designed To Work

If you look around into the world you are a part of, you will see evidence of how life is wonderful and beautiful, yes, and also evidence that many aspects of life are not working. In fact, you may find more evidence to say life is not working than to say it is. So many people are uncomfortable and suffering. Who could say that life works? And yet, it does.

Life works.

If you don't believe me, if you don't see life working, look at life itself. You sure don't have to look far to witness the perfection of life. Take a walk in nature. Pick one small expression of the life you find there and study it. Whether it is a tree, a leaf, a flower, a bird, or some other life in nature, take time to look at it closely. Focus on it, observe its perfection, its beauty. Look around you and notice children laughing and people smiling.

So many pieces are working together for this manifestation of life working so well to occur. And not just life, but the Universe around life is working, planets are turning, the sun comes up in the morning.

Nature and the Universe

are
working
so very well.

Yet when we look at the world we live in, things appear to be spiraling out of control. Everywhere we see problems, things like global warming, raging wars, inequity of wealth, depletion of resources. And we see conflicting, even fighting, between people, families, groups, countries, and between loved ones, strangers – between friends and enemies – rich people and welfare recipients, democrats and republicans, meat eaters and vegetarians, native born people and immigrants – the list goes on and on.

However, the conflict we feel in the world around us, in the world outside ourselves, reflects the conflict within us. If we are experiencing an inner conflict, this is because we are at war with ourselves. In that moment we are not able to tune in to the reality that: everything is working; we are part of a Universe that works; and life is designed to work.

11
You ARE Designed to Work

You are part of the flow of life, therefore you are designed to work too. This may not be an idea you have spent time contemplating, so give yourself a chance to think about this, to get used to the idea. Start with this understanding: It is not logical to say that everything in this Universe is perfectly designed except for you.

You are part of nature. You are a vehicle for the expression of life. You are part of the spirit of life and part of the perfectly working Universe. You are a part of creation. You live in the flow that is all around you, the flow of life, and of the Universe. You and the flow are one, there is no separation.

You are
in the flow of life
as much as is anyone else.

Yet if nature is designed to work and we are designed to work, then how come our world and our lives sometimes do not seem to us to be working? Good question. Where is the disconnect?

The disconnect is this: We get off track through misunderstanding what is going on, by thinking what is being said *around us* is being said *within us*. We confuse what is said outside with what is said on the inside, deep inside ourselves. We mistake *messages coming at us from the outside world* for the *true messages we are giving ourselves*, the ones coming from our authentic selves. So we can miss the truth, our truth.

We can misunderstand something which is not our truth and think it is THE truth, OUR truth, our AUTHENTIC TRUTH.

When we are living inside of this misunderstanding, we may not realize this in full. Instead we may be conflicted and afraid – afraid of the conflict between what the outside world is telling us is true and what we know is true for us.

You do know what is true for you, your truth, because you are designed to know, to feel the truth, the authentic truth. You are designed to work.

While we are unclear about which is our own truth and which is what the outside world tells us is true, we live in fear. We live as false selves, fearful false selves. We believe we have to compromise to survive. So we compromise, we live as compromised selves.

When this is happening, we are not able to fully value ourselves because we are not being ourselves. What we are not valuing is the person we are being, the person the outside world is telling us to be. When we contemplate the idea of fully valuing ourselves, we may feel that our own true value can be taken away from us. But nothing and no one can take your true value away from you....

The purpose of this book is not to try and solve all the world's problems. However, the principles are generally the same whether we are looking at global situations or into our own personal lives. For now, we are just going to focus on you having the realization that you are designed to work.

Once you have an understanding of the wholeness and perfection that you are, your presence will ripple out and support others in having this realization of who they truly are. When people understand the beauty and truth of who they are, this will be reflected in the world. Life evolves from the inside out.

Just like the flowers, trees and animals, you have been designed for a purpose. You came into this world with energy that vibrates at a specific pitch. When your thoughts, words and actions harmonize with this pitch, you are operating at full capacity and sharing the gift that you are.

You experience a feeling of great satisfaction and fulfillment that is so profound that it is indescribable.

When a rose is placed in good soil, fed and nurtured with the proper amount of sunlight, it flourishes. Why, because it is designed to bloom. It wants to bloom. It is its nature to bloom. In fact, the more you trim and cut away the branches that have lived out their usefulness, the more the roses bloom. In the right environment, year after year the roses will bloom.

You may be saying, well that isn't me because I was brought up in the wrong environment and my circumstances were less than ideal. Therefore I can't bloom to my full potential. This is where the misunderstanding enters. You see, unlike a rose, you have a conscious awareness. Your consciousness can choose the bigger yes and can choose to live as your authentic self. You do live within your physical environment, but more than this you live within your consciousness.

And, your thoughts are your own. You have absolute dominion over your thoughts. No one has the power to cause you to believe something that is not true. When you know your truth, you know your authentic self.

You are designed to live an authentic life. You are designed to work.

Your environment and circumstances may not have been the most supportive for you up to this point, but you are neither your environment nor your circumstances. You are bigger and more powerful than both. Your life is lived from the inside out.

You are designed to be the expression of the life that you are.

No one and no thing can change that. Let me back track a moment as this is not exactly true. There is someone who could prevent you from being the fullest expression of life that you are – and that someone is you. No one but you has the power to stop you from living as your authentic self. But through a misunderstanding of who you are, by listening to the noise all around you and to your false self, you have the free will to block your good.

You block your good when you decide, usually unconsciously or by default, to live as your compromised self. Fortunately you also have the power to listen within and be guided by your true self.

If you want to know the meaning of your life, who you are here to be, what you are here to do and have, then tune in and listen for the harmony of your life. When you follow the vibration you are feeling, the vibration of you, your life will be meaningful both to you and to the people around you. By becoming familiar with how your energy wants to flow, your path will light up.

Through the 5 Step process presented in this book, you will learn how to align your consciousness with your authentic self to be who you really are.

12
Finding Your Place in the Flow

Personal fulfillment and the authentic happiness this brings is your birthright. This is yours and therefore something you can always have access to. However, before you can tap into this wellspring of happiness, you do have to learn how to work with your energy.

If your energy is currently weighted toward not being fully you, toward a sense of less-than you, of scarcity, then you are not tapping into your full power. And this affects how you feel about your life. You may find yourself running around, working very hard to get yourself back into balance, trying to feel better about yourself and your life, and yet it all still feels futile.

Bringing yourself naturally back into balance is the way to reclaim yourself, your authentic self. The problem is that we are not taught to do this. Most of us have never been told anything about this issue of reclaiming our authentic selves, let alone how to do this.

Instead, education, communities, families, advertising, social behaviors that include comparing ourselves with others, all lead us to believe that what we want lives outside of ourselves. We are led to believe that all we have to do is grab the brass ring and then we will be happy.

If we believe happiness comes from the outside in, we will try to please our communities and families, we will attempt to buy the perfect product such as a car or dress or house, or to have the perfect career. We will follow the rules.

All this is about looking outside ourselves for meaning, fulfillment, happiness with life. And ultimately this does not work.

**Happiness is an inside job:
inside you.**

And you can reclaim your authentic self and have the authentic true happiness that you deserve. This is what this book is talking about. Initially, the *5 Steps to An Authentically Happy Life* you find in this book serve as training wheels to help you understand how the different aspects of who you are work together.

Eventually, you will be able to kick off the training wheels and guide yourself. You will come to experience first hand the wholeness and perfection that you are. This process has helped me and my clients realize that there is nothing missing in my life, nor in their lives. Just keep telling yourself:

**I have what I need
to be who I am.**

There is a current of love that permeates life, all life. We have all felt it at one time or another. It may have been during those poignant moments, special occasions, listening to music, watching a movie.

Or maybe you have felt this feeling when you were with loved ones. It is that pleasant feeling that all is right with the world. You feel loved and secure.

Being in this flow, this current, gives you a heightened sense of awareness. You are able to see beyond the chaos and feel the harmony of life. This current of harmony and love is available to us at any moment, but we have to know how to access it. Through this 5 Step process, you will be able to swim in this current whenever you want. Being in this flow you get the sense that you are part of something bigger than your survival consciousness. And you are. When you say yes to this current, this energy that is calling you forth, you grow and expand – and we all grow and expand along with you.

This flow you are part of is like an unformed love, unformed until you mold it. Your thoughts, feelings, words, and actions shape your life. How you receive and give the gift of your life is up to you. You are part of the expansion of the Universe. We are all part of the expansion of the Universe.

If you are on the planet, you are part of the flow of life. However, just because you are alive doesn't mean you have an awareness of your place in the flow, or of the flow at all.

Take a moment to think about yourself. Who are you?

The answer may come to you quickly and with certainty: I know who I am because the world around me tells me who I am. Yes, sometimes we believe we are who the world – the people, the organizations, the activities, the beliefs around us – say who we are. And sometimes what we hear about ourselves from the world around us is pretty right on.

Or is it? Can the outside world really be in charge of telling our inner selves about ourselves? Quite often, we are filled with a lingering sense that what we are told we are is not exactly who we are, and maybe is not at all who we are. We are not always sure what to make of this feeling. Many of us try to ignore it, or to hear only bits of it.

You are the gatekeeper to your experience of the flow. Your life experience runs through the filters of your thoughts. Are you listening to and allowing for the harmony of who you are, or are you tuning this out?

The harmony you are is specific and unique to you.

There is a flow you were born into, and you can feel this flow by the pull of your energy. Just as a musician receives inspiration and then writes the musical notes on paper, once you connect with the harmony in your mind you can create this harmony in your world.

If we don't know ourselves, life can feel random and confusing. We don't know where to look, who to be, or what to do. Without clarity regarding who we are, our minds drift into a consciousness of scarcity. When we're scared and confused we want guarantees. Our attention becomes focused on our survival instead of on our contribution.

Instead of fully participating in the giving and receiving flow of life, our actions are conditional. Our giving becomes tit for tat. "I'll give but I'd better be rewarded." "I'll make this investment of time and energy but it better pay off." Not trusting the flow of life has us feeling guarded and separate.

When we feel separate from the flow we can feel as if we don't have access to this flow, this very flow we are already part of. And at times we may feel as if the flow has gone away and abandoned us, as if this flow is no longer within our reach. Even though we may think the flow has grown restricted, this restriction of the flow is not possible because …

the flow
does not constrict.

The only thing that is constricting is our AWARENESS of our being part of the flow, our awareness of life energy flowing through us, our awareness of the abundance of the flow. This is why, when we feel this way, when we feel that we are stuck, limited, constricted, there is a part of us that is confused. Deep inside we do know we are connected to the flow, but in the moment we may feel separate from it.

This sense of separation can feel quite unsettling and yet very real. When you feel this way, part of your mind is letting itself believe that you really are disconnected from the flow, from life. The resulting confusion, frustration, fear, pain, and sense of constriction is a perception of, a pocket of …

scarcity.

Do not be concerned. You can move from this confused self to your authentic self. As you learn to listen and follow the guidance of your authentic self, you will gracefully be brought into the current, into the flow of your life.

PART THREE

13 Awakening To Your Authentic Self

For a long time now, there has been a lot of talk about what is called the authentic self. Yet we may not know exactly what that means because becoming aware of the authentic self is a work in progress.

Your authentic self is ready and waiting to be recognized by you. As your awareness deepens, you are able to see and experience more of your authentic self. With your growing clarity about yourself, you will find that your life becomes richer and more satisfying. More of the energy and love that you are can be revealed as your facades and fears fade. Your authentic self is continuously at work seeking to be expressed, or sending you signals about not wanting to be ignored or suppressed.

I want to say more about this authentic self we all have within us, but first let me talk a little about the many theories of self and authentic self. I will not go into all of these here, but I do want to briefly note a few aspects of theories and philosophies of what are called "authenticity" and the "authentic self." The term *authenticity* is found in psychology where it is defined as the degree to which a person is true to her or his own personality or character despite outside external pressures not to be.

The field of philosophy has also looked at authenticity, discussing the way the external world impacts the inner self, the sense of self, the way one can be true to oneself, the definition of self and of true self, and the negative aspects of inauthentic living. Many theorists including sociologists have discussed the notion of selling out rather than being true to oneself. And throughout many of these discussions is the concept that being authentic, or true to oneself, is challenging and frequently a difficult path to follow.

I will not take issue with some of the greatest minds in history who have tackled the idea of authenticity. I will however say that the steps, the *5 Steps to An Authentically Happy Life* that you find on the following pages, are not major hurdles. You will not find the process of becoming more authentic difficult. Why would this be difficult? You have been with yourself since birth. You know yourself. The question becomes are you going to admit to yourself that you know.

When you know yourself
you know life.

When you know life
you know the flow of life.

When you know the flow
you know its goodness and
how you are part of this.

When you know the goodness
that lives within you
you also know the goodness
that lives within everyone else.

When you have faith in
what lives within you
you have faith in the flow.

Having faith in ourselves and in the flow opens us to the giving and receiving flow. Instead of sitting on the sidelines observing and withholding the gift that we are, we trust the flow and become participants in life.

When you are living as your authentic self, people feel safe and good in your presence. They like who they are when they are with you. Your authenticity shines the light on their authenticity and gives them the courage to let their light shine too. They appreciate who they are in your presence. This inspires them to choose their bigger yes and share the gift that they are.

This is why knowing and living as your true self instead of as your compromised self is a gift for everyone. You end up spreading happiness wherever you go. This is the farthest thing from being selfish.

Actually, it could be said we are living selfishly when we live as our compromised selves instead of as our true, our authentic, selves. The love that we are is being withheld. However this is because we are unaware of the way we are living. We are not realizing we are not allowing our authentic selves to come through. And if we are unaware, then we don't really have a choice, we don't really know better.

Living from the compromised self
is usually
not done intentionally.

We do this when we don't know
there is another way.

As you learn more about your authentic self and how to be this self, you will be more aware of yourself. You may find that you are being your compromised self at times and being your true self at other times.

This process is a moment by moment thing. Sometimes you may feel your connection to life, and other times you may feel separate, not part of life.

As you learn the *5 Steps to An Authentically Happy Life,* you will spend more and more time living as your authentic self. Yes, there will be times you will fall off the horse, fall away from your authentic self, but you will always know how to get back on, back to yourself. And this will put you more and more in touch with the giving and receiving flow, with benefits such as these:

1. The quality of your life will greatly improve.
2. You will feel more at peace with yourself and the world.
3. You will have the satisfaction of living a life well lived.
4. You will have the satisfaction of knowing you are giving the gift you came here to give.
5. You will be able to live an authentically happy life.

You need never fear that you will not be able to live your values and be your authentic self. What you are lives within you always, as long as you are alive (and possibly beyond, depending on your belief system). No one can take your values from you. To live your values, you must simply acknowledge and claim them. Claiming the gift that you are allows you to live an authentic life and to follow the path of your own personal evolution.

It's easy to feel you are not part of the flow and don't deserve to be here. When you find yourself feeling people don't get you, or that people perceive you to be someone other than who you are, you are left feeling not seen or heard.

We start to feel invisible and very often drift into the "nothing matters, I don't matter, nothing I do matters" mode. These thoughts leave us feeling less than satisfied and not fully alive. So right now you can check in and examine how fully you are participating in the giving and receiving flow.

Ask yourself:

What portion of my day is spent
living authentically
versus

going through the motions of who I think I should be?

Some of you will recognize that a large portion of your day is spent living authentically. If this is you, then the steps I share in this book will help you make this experience even richer for yourself. We can always go deeper into living an authentic and happy life.

If, on the other hand, only a small fraction of your day is spent living authentically, then you have a lot to look forward to. Your life is waiting to be received and lived by you. You will see that:

You are
perfectly designed
to be who you truly are,
to live the life you love.

We are all
designed this way.

What this means is your success has already been granted to you. The answers to questions about who are you and what are you here to do are within you. Success is living life in the way that resonates with your own true nature. One life is not more important than another. We each have a unique gift that we came here to share. If you withhold your energy and share just a fraction of who you truly are, the world misses out on your gift. So do you.

Of course life will go on if your gift, your essence, is withheld. But the experience of being alive will be less than it could be for you and for the people you share your life with.

You are here to share the gift that you are. Fortunately, you have been given a personalized blueprint to know what constitutes a meaningful life for you. The answers are yours to hear and to know about yourself.

To be your true self you do not want someone else telling you who to be or what to do with your life. You want the answer to originate from the source of your being. You want to hear *yourself* tell *you* this. You want the answer to come from within you.

As your consciousness deepens and expands, you will find you are ever more aware that there is a you there, the highest form of you that you can know at the moment you are knowing. Becoming intimate with your life is an exciting process. Every step of the way brings you insight and energy.

Ultimately there is no limit to the depth with which you can receive your life. The answers are within you.

You are one with an infinite source of wisdom, intelligence and love that communicates to you your relationship to the flow. When you are focused in the direction of your true self, you feel an energy calling you forth. As you move in that direction, move through your thoughts, words, and actions, your energy lightens and you feel a sense of expansiveness and freedom.

When you are focused on thoughts or taking actions that are not in alignment with your true self, you are turned away from the flow and your energy becomes heavy. You feel a sense of resistance and probably some anger and frustration. Instead of dancing with the flow of life you have the feeling of trying to swim against a current. This can be painful and exhausting.

Learn to discern between these two energies within you, the energies of both the authentic self and the compromised self. Sensing the difference will reveal answers to you, information you can use to live a fulfilling authentic life, a life you love.

If you don't see the answers you carry within you, know that you will soon. Just work with the *5 Steps to An Authentically Happy Life* you read on the following pages. Once you do, you will find that you are no longer blocked, stuck.

This is a book about getting *unstuck* ....

What will naturally follow your shift in awareness is an expanded ability to experience and appreciate the physical plane. This includes a greater flow of creative expression and a new peace of mind.

If you feel like your life is going nowhere, or that you are always working hard but still spinning your wheels, just know that there is a way through all this.

14
Moving from Stuck to Flowing

None of us like to feel stuck. When we don't feel our connection to life, when we feel separate and cut off from life, we become anxious and grow quite discombobulated. We start taking any action, even if it is destructive, just to feel alive.

**Whether or not you are aware of this,
you are connected to all of life.
We all are.**

If you are breathing, you are a part of the whole. However, your experience of life can vary depending upon your choices and how you perceive your relationship to life. If you feel powerless to affect your life circumstances, you may sit on the sidelines waiting for your turn, feeling anger, frustration, or apathy brewing deep inside you. Or maybe you jump into action suddenly hoping to catch a lucky break by proving your worth.

**If you want to be truly happy,
you have to connect with *your* life.**

You cannot experience what you want when you are feeling separate from life. Of course I'm not saying you "should" reconnect to life or you won't get what you want. Rather, I know you want to feel at one with life because that is what you are.

We are truly happy when we feel the energy within us connecting with the energy around us. It's like breathing. We may be okay holding our breath for a few seconds, but it's not going to take very long before something has to give.

When our personal thoughts are not aligned with the thoughts of life, we feel stuck. We may have all the justifications and reasons for why we feel stuck, but if our energy isn't flowing, we feel this and feeling this makes us unhappy. The reason why this makes us unhappy is because we know something is off.

We are not designed to feel separate, diminished or less than. The good news is that it actually takes more energy to be stuck than to be flowing. And with a shift in awareness our energy moves instantly.

Moving from a sense of feeling limited and not able to fully express, to a sense of being part of the giving and receiving flow of life, is available to all of us. Moving into feeling part of the flow is easier than you may think. This is not only easier, it is also a much more fun way to go through life.

If your energy has been stuck, you have been working too hard, pushing too hard against your authentic self. You can think of this movement toward happiness as a movement along a continuum, moving from stuck to flowing, from fear to faith, something like this:

STUCK → → → → → → → FLOWING

Which is actually something more like this:

From → → → → → → → → → → → *To*

NOT BEING AWARE THAT YOU ARE IN THE FLOW	**BEING AWARE THAT YOU ARE AN INTEGRAL PART OF THE FLOW**

We feel stuck when we are resisting the flow. We resist the flow when we can't find our place in it. We can't find our place in it when we are looking through the lens of our compromised self. Our judgments about ourselves keep us feeling separate from the rest of life and distort our perception of life. It is as if we are living in a fog and can't see beyond it. Our clarity is deeply impaired when we are feeling stuck and separate from life.

We are all within the flow at all times. However, participating fully in the giving and receiving flow involves being aware that you are in this flow and that you deserve to be here.

15
Knowing the Flow As the Path To Ourselves

We are the gatekeepers to our experience of the flow. Every moment of every day we are either saying yes to our authentic selves or yes to our compromised selves. These are choices we are making on an ongoing basis. As we do this, we communicate our choices to ourselves and to the world via our energy and our words and actions. However, without an awareness of how we are flowing our energy, our experience of life can look to others and to ourselves haphazard and unpredictable.

Deciding how you want to flow your energy and learning how to consciously allow your energy to flow is your path to authentic happiness. This is both a very large concept and a very simple one. There is a part of you that intuitively knows how to flow your energy and another part of you that has forgotten that you know. But no need to be over concerned. You are perfectly designed to know the flow and to tune into it so that you can be who you truly are.

You are designed to do this,
to know and be you.

I use the word "flow" to describe the energy that permeates all life. It is the invisible behind the visible: the energy that sparks creativity, grows plants, keeps our hearts beating, holds the planets in place. The source of all life has its origin in this energy that I refer to as flow.

You are in the flow
and the flow is in you.

You may want to substitute the word flow with a word that resonates for you. When we talk about being one with the flow, you may want to say being one with God or one with Source, Spirit, Love, Life, Divine Wisdom, Goodness, or the Energy of all that is. You choose the way you want to label this flow.

There is no place where this energy is not. We either turn toward it and embrace it, or we turn away from it and limit our experience of it.

16
There is Wisdom In Your Resistance

If you are not feeling the flow you are a part of, this indicates that you have run into some resistance. Resistance arises from engaging in thoughts that diminish you while you feel the block these thoughts are placing, even when not understanding in full what this block is.

Messages that block you come at you, and you repeat these messages to yourself. You may hear messages trying to convince you that you are less than who you are, telling you that you are doing something wrong trying to be your authentic self or any part of your authentic self.

All resistance is based on a sense of scarcity. This scarcity says that it is not okay to be who you truly are because there is something inherently wrong with the way you are.

Resistance arises from within.
When we have a misunderstanding
of our value
and of our place in the flow,
we get stuck.

Being stuck is not necessarily a bad thing. It alerts us that there is a better more satisfying way to go through life than we are currently living. The resistance we feel is alerting us that, in this moment, our thoughts are engaged in a misunderstanding of our worth.

Thank goodness for the resistance. If we aren't feeling this resistance, we aren't able to know what thoughts are keeping us from experiencing the flow. Our resistance alerts us to the moments when we sell out on ourselves.

When we are feeling resistance, this resistance is an indication that something is going on inside us: we are feeling pulled in a different direction from the one the outside world is telling us we should go. We feel pulled to be our authentic selves yet we are having a difficult time finding our way back into the flow. Messages from the outside world are blocking us and we are compromising by following those "should" messages we are hearing.

You will become more aware of what this experience is. And, as you move through the *5 Steps to An Authentically Happy Life* presented in this book, you will learn to see and to appreciate the wisdom in resistance.

Know that when we are stuck, we are expending a tremendous amount of energy trying to get unstuck but not getting unstuck. Instead of growing and waking up to the fullness of who we are, we are participating in life with the brakes on.

This behavior leads us into the jerky moments in our lives, the ups and downs, the alls or nothings, the excess dramas. This action is not necessarily bad, as it can be quite informative. Of course, if all this up and down drama continues for an extended period of time it can be exhausting and wear us down. When this is going on, we can miss out on the life we came here to live.

Being more aware of the ups and downs, the waves we ride, and of the pushes and pulls we feel, gives us important information about tuning into the flow that is all around us and within us at all times.

Instead of cresting and crashing, we can tune into our natural rhythm and be at peace with who we are. We can spot our resistance and learn from it. Experiencing our resistance actually supports us in finding our place in the flow.

If we look, we can see and know when and where we limit ourselves, when we are staying stuck instead of fully living our lives. Our resistance brings us to the exact spot where we are feeling separate from the flow. Finding where our energy is stuck is not difficult. However, just because we have clarity as to where our flow feels constricted, we don't just magically get back to participating in the giving and receiving flow. We have to understand what is going on to change it, and this is what this book is all about.

We will explore the topic of resistance further in Step 4: UNDERSTANDING YOUR RESISTANCE, but just know for now that you are perfectly designed to live a rich and satisfying life. All of your feelings and emotions, both positive and negative, are here to support you in discovering your path of true satisfaction.

17
Your Path to A Happy Life

Think about who you believe you are today, at this moment in your life. How would you describe yourself? Would you start with what you are to the people around you: I'm a mom, sister, friend – or with what you do: I'm an engineer, dancer, pastry chef, runner – or with what you own: I'm a homeowner, car owner. Or would you define yourself by your personality traits: I'm funny, serious, kind, talkative, energetic, judgmental, sloppy, etc. While these might be descriptions that fit in some way, none of these is what you are.

Neither what you are to others, nor what you own, nor what you do, nor your personality traits are you. Rather these are the surface you, the you defined by the outside world. These are not the true you.

The true you I am talking about here is the authentic you. This is who you truly are, deep down inside. You are comprised of energy, energy and a flow we might want to describe as pure love.

What is this love I am talking about here? This love is more than the every day, "I am in love with" or "I just love to eat sweets" or this sort of surface love. Here, I am talking about authentic, sheer and pure love. This love is a positive bursting forth of energy and creation. When you feel love for anything or anyone, you are expressing some of this greater love. Every day love experiences help you tap into this greater love.

When you are tuning into this pure love you carry within you, then this love emanates from you and touches everyone you come in contact with. This is why this love is infectious in a good way, is attractive to people around you. The energy of this love is the essence of what and who you are. And, living as your authentic self you will live the love that you are in your own unique way.

You can test this theory right now. Imagine yourself embracing something or someone you love, whether it is your pet, your partner, your child, a project, an instrument, a painting, a food, or an idea. Notice the flow of energy that travels from you toward the object of your affection. You can feel the energy within you expand when your attention is focused on what you love.

Yet when you doubt yourself and question whether or not it is safe or right to be the love that you are or to love what you love, you can feel your energy constrict. It is as if you just put the brakes on yourself. Notice the energy it takes to keep these brakes on, to withhold who you are and the love that you are. The energy that wants to be expressed is being thwarted.

When we believe we can't be who we are, this can feel as if we are in a battle with the world and the people in it. Think about this.

Even though this may seem to you to be about everyone else, you are really in a battle with yourself when this is going on. You are looking for some relief, a place to lay the blame for your unhappiness. If you can't find a way to be the *who* that you are and the *love* that you are, you feel blocked, stuck.

You see, you are designed to grow, to expand and express your energy and love. If your energy can't find a way through you, cannot be expressed by you, then you are not authentically happy. And think about this:

Being the love that you are is your path to a happy life. You will come to see that your deepest desire is to be your authentic self. And your biggest fear is that you can't be who you truly are.

Until you learn how to consciously align with the flow of your energy, your attention may be drifting places you don't want it to go. This sensation may simply take the form of being tired a lot. Or you may find other signs that your energy is being restricted. Maybe you just cannot understand why you feel bored, frustrated, or have lost your zest for life.

Eventually, you may want to ask yourself: where am I expending my energy?

**What portion of my energy
is spent each day
on what I love?**

Do you know the answer to this? Have you ever felt afraid to even ask the question because you were fearful of what the answer may be? Do not be concerned.

You can decide for yourself when you are ready to ask yourself this sort of question, when you really do want to know. Just keep in mind that you do have a right to want to ask yourself this.

**After all,
this is *your* life.**

18
You are Perfectly Designed To Live The Life You Love

Just as the flower releases its fragrant scent, your heart longs to express its true essence. When you follow your heart's desire, what is revealed is the essence of who you are. Your essence matches your desires.

The life you desire to live
wants to be lived by you.
There is no separation.

Your consciousness would not register a desire if there were not a deep inner nudging calling you to be and do. When you respond to this desire and take action in the direction of the inspiration you are receiving, your life begins to reflect your heart's desire.

The reason you are perfectly designed to live the life you love is because you are the one who receives the desire to live your own life. This is about you, about who you really are. This is not about anyone else.

You see, no two people are receiving the same exact inspiration. No one but you is receiving the desire to live *your* life. That is why there is no competition when living as your authentic self. There is not another person on this planet who has the same combination of values and desires as you do.

This particular expression of your authentic self, of this unique expression of self and love, can come into your awareness. This is yours to claim, to express and to follow. You will know more and more that you are indeed perfectly designed.

Furthermore, you are perfectly designed to do one thing: to live the life you love. If you are not living the life you love, you are finding out how to, or you are feeling somewhere deep inside a great longing to.

PART FOUR

19
About the Steps

It is now time to dive into the 5 Steps so you can experience first hand what I am talking about. Let the fun begin.

LET'S START HERE

You are a very special, unique expression of life. There are no two of you. Once you accept this, you can see that your very own particular happiness is your very own particular happiness.

Your own path to happiness is not going to look like anyone else's. What brings joy to one person may be neutral or even a burden to another. Your joy, your happiness, is something only you can know directly because it is yours. Others may enjoy being around your joy, however they are experiencing this indirectly. Every person has the potential to directly experience his or her own joy.

RECLAIM YOUR TRUE HAPPINESS

And, your very own particular happiness originates from you living as your very own authentic self. The more you are living as your authentic self, the more authentically happy you will be.

You carry your own true happiness with you, within you. All that is required to be authentically happy, to feel the purest happiness, is to:

reclaim your own life,
which is already yours.

YOUR OWN AUTHENTIC PATH

The 5 Steps to your authentic self and life are simple. You can begin this journey today. Do so, and you will immediately begin to feel a shift in your energy. By working these steps you will begin to release your compromised self, the person you were taught to be or believed you should be. This definition of your self came from outside you.

The true you comes from within you. This makes sense, doesn't it? After all, you are not what the world around you says you should be, will be, must be.

When you release your compromised self, you create more room for your authentic self. Once you rediscover your authentic self, your authentic self can come out of hiding, and you will once again be you. This reclaiming of yourself brings you back to the joy, your own authentic joy, of being alive.

WORKING WITH THESE STEPS

Working with these steps is a process. This is a process of looking inside to find out who you really are. From there, the process moves into your making decisions that align your thoughts, words and actions with your authentic self.

As you take this look inside, you will find in there all sorts of important and interesting information about yourself. You will discover what you actually do value, what you actually do want. You will also learn where you get stopped and why. Sometimes when offered the opportunity to reveal ourselves, to be our authentic selves, we hold back. Frequently we are feeling fear on some level, fear of following the path of our true selves. But let this fear stand off to the side. There is so much to be discovered, so much of yourself to find.

The 5 Steps on the following pages serve as a roadmap. Follow this map, these 5 Steps, to transport yourself from fear of knowing your true self, to the joy of knowing yourself, of being you. Have faith in this process of revealing your authentic self, faith that knowing your true self is the absolute best option in life for you. This is the best option because once you know who you really are, you are free to live the life you came here to live.

Let me say a little more here about the fear of knowing who you truly are. Sometimes we are afraid of really looking at ourselves; we think we are going to find something within ourselves that we are ashamed of or won't like.

However, do not be concerned about this. Knowing yourself, finding your authentic self, doesn't work this way. There is nothing in this process of reclaiming yourself to be afraid of. You are not going to find anything within your true self that you do not love. What you may not be crazy about is the compromised self you thought you had to become, should become, or perhaps had been led to believe you already were.

Each time you travel the journey from fear of yourself to faith in yourself, your consciousness expands. Your faith in life and in the flow of, the spirit of, life expands. You will come to realize that there is never a time when you are not being held and guided by your higher, most authentic self. So welcome to this journey, the journey guided by these ***5 Steps to An Authentically Happy Life***:

Step 1: Becoming Aware
Step 2: Revealing Your Values
Step 3: Recognizing Your Desires
Step 4: Understanding Your Resistance
Step 5: Choosing Your Bigger Yes

THE IMPORTANCE OF KEEPING YOUR OWN BIGGER YES JOURNAL

Revealing your authentic self is a process. The 5 Steps you are working with in this book take you on the journey to your authentic self which is the only place you are going to find true and lasting happiness. This is not a book to sit back and passively read, although of course you can do that if you want. However, if you want to live more fully as your authentic self, you will have work to do. But rest assured, the focus and attention you bring to this work will be reflected in the quality of your life. Your life will transform.

Throughout this process you will be gathering and analyzing data to reveal your authentic self. This is a step by step process that builds upon itself. It is a cumulative process. Think of yourself as a scientist or as a researcher. You are going to be gathering data and it is your job to digest and make sense of what you have collected.

No one else is going to be working with your pieces other than you. No one has your answers other than you. You will want a journal to record your findings so you can gain a deeper understanding of your true, your authentic self, and so you can continue this process throughout your life, or as long as you want to during your life.

As we move to new levels of personal consciousness, we can forget where we were before our awareness expanded to each new level. Our minds tend to lose the details of our journeys, to forget where we have come from. It will be good and satisfying for you to keep track of your journey. Be sure to start and keep entering items into your:

Bigger Yes Journal.

This journaling is important. It will help you know where you have been to better know where you are going. I encourage you to start a *Bigger Yes Journal*. Use it to record your daily states of mind, understandings, and insights as you go through this process. Also use your journal to make notes as you read this book, and as you work with these 5 Steps and their exercises. Be sure you date each of your journal entries. Also be sure to label your exercise material and lists with subject, title, and date as this book suggests. Later, and likely again and again over time, you will want to go back over what you have recorded in your journal, and to tie all your information together.

This journal is certainly going to be a great record for you. It will remind you that you have travelled substantial ground. And, it will encourage you to keep going, to always keep going.

Once you get into the habit of ***choosing your bigger yes*** in your daily life and of celebrating the results that follow, you will not want to go back to choosing your lesser yes. This journal will bring clarity to the choices you make as you move forward. It will be a record of the beautiful unfolding of your authentic self. You will see your own personal evolution as you look over your journal.

The 5 Steps charted on the following page will give you an idea of the journey you are about to embark upon. By recording your journey you will begin to see patterns and themes in your life. These will provide you with greater clarity regarding who you are and what you want. You will find yourself understanding yourself more every day. Your journal will reflect back to you the natural rhythm and progress of your life. Your journal is the record of your journey to:

YOU.

CHARTING THE 5 STEPS TO YOUR BIGGER YES

The following chart lists these 5 Steps to your bigger yes, to your authentic self. These steps will lead you on the path to your authentic life. You will see here, in the third column, a brief note about each of these steps. And in the fourth column, you will see listed the name of the exercise for each step. All of this will be explained on the following pages, step by step.

	Name of This Step	**About This Step**	**Exercise Used In This Step**
1	Becoming Aware	The first step to living an authentic life is to become more aware of yourself.	Seeing My Push-es/Pulls Exercise
2	Revealing Your Values	Then you can reveal to yourself who you are, who your authentic self is.	Revealing My Values Exercise
3	Recognizing Your Desires	Knowing this, you can then follow your true desires, those of your authentic self.	Recognizing My Desires Exercise
4	Understand-ing Your Resistance	You will become able to see and understand where you experience resistance to you being your authentic self.	Understanding My Resistance Exercise
5	Choosing Your Bigger Yes	Once you have the in-creased clarity of the first four steps, you can **Choose Your Big-ger YES** in your life. You can align your thoughts, words and actions with your au-thentic self.	Choosing My Bigger Yes Exercise

20
Step One: Becoming Aware

STEP 1: BECOMING AWARE is the first step in the process of living your authentic life. But, what is it that you are becoming aware of? You are becoming aware of the brilliance, beauty and truth of who you are. You are learning to listen to your inner wisdom.

The language of Spirit, of your authentic self, is communicating with you and letting you know the degree to which you are sharing or withholding your true self – withholding your true self from yourself and from the world. To answer these questions, you will want to ask yourself whether you are going with, moving with, the current of your life or are resisting it.

Take the journey of becoming aware and receive the richness of your life.

You can develop a heightened awareness of yourself and of your life. Becoming aware is an ongoing journey from not knowing to knowing. For many of us, this is a journey from feeling powerless to feeling powerful, from feeling fear to feeling faith in ourselves and faith in the spirit of life.

You can move:

From not knowing, not being aware →
to knowing, being aware.

From feeling powerless →
to feeling powerful.

From feeling fear →→→
to feeling faith in yourself
and in the spirit of life.

THE PUSHES AND PULLS YOU ARE FEELING

On this Step 1 journey of becoming aware, you begin to recognize the pushes and pulls you are experiencing and what these pushes and pulls are communicating to you. Recognizing these pushes and pulls will help you become more aware of yourself and of what is going on within you.

You are an individualized expression of Spirit, of Life. Therefore your pushes and pulls will be unique to you. What may be a pull for you could be a push for someone else and vice versa. You feel yourself being pulled when you are energized, enthusiastic and moving with the current of your life.

On the other hand, when you feel yourself pushing against things, you are not moving with the current of your life. This pushing against is really pushing against yourself. You will come to see this, you will come to know when it feels like you can't be your authentic self and live your own life.

Your pushes and pulls are the barometer of your relationship to the flow, of your relationship with yourself. These pushes and pulls reveal to you how you are currently flowing your energy. You can feel when you are allowing yourself to be pulled by the flow of life and when you are pushing, resisting the flow.

Perhaps you feel a pull when you are working in your garden or singing, or doing something you love to do. Your pulls may include your being drawn to a book or a movie or putting together a business deal.

Your pulls are guiding you into the giving and receiving flow and calling forth the expression of your authentic self.

You will want to become highly sensitive to, very aware of, both the pushes and the pulls you are experiencing. With practice, discerning between a push and a pull will become easy for you. When people first start working with their pushes and pulls, they want their list of pushes and pulls to be comprised mostly of their pulls, of the things they feel best about. However, once you have been working with your pushes and pulls awhile, you will see the tremendous value in your pushes.

Your pushes tell you a lot about yourself. In fact, your pushes can lead you to many of your pulls. You see, all of your as of yet unfulfilled desires, the desires you have not yet allowed yourself to live out, are on the other side of your pushes. Your pushes take you right there, right to the place where you are resisting your own good. So your pushes are quite valuable. Do not be afraid to look at them, to acknowledge they exist.

There is also great value in your pulls. Your pulls are the energy of your truest, most authentic self. These pulls are calling you forth. You are becoming aware of your true self and of its most authentic drives, callings, values, and desires. We will say more about these aspects of the authentic self in the following steps. For now, let's stay focused on this BECOMING AWARE step, Step 1.

Awareness is such an important part of the process of your own personal evolution. In fact, awareness is essential in this process. Awareness heals and reunites you with your wholeness. Having a heightened awareness of the energy that you are is essential.

**This awareness
is a journey in itself:
the journey of the self
to its
most authentic version.**

LISTEN TO THE ENERGY OF YOUR AUTHENTIC SELF

As you become ever more aware of yourself, you will notice your awareness deepening day by day and moment by moment. This is the ideal to strive for: ever deepening awareness.

It is now time to listen to the energy of your authentic self. You can do this by doing the *SEEING MY PUSHES/PULLS EXERCISE* on the coming pages. This is an exercise you will want to do again and again as you embrace the idea of your own personal evolution and happiness. This exercise will help you to:

Fine tune
your awareness of
your
pushes
and your
pulls…

and
therefore
your awareness of
yourself.

To get started on this, take the time to look quite closely at your pushes and pulls. Let's look first at the actual differences between your pushes and your pulls.

THINKING ABOUT THE PUSHES AND PULLS YOU EXPERIENCE

"Is this thing, or this activity I'm engaged in, or this idea I'm thinking about, causing me to feel a push or a pull?" Good question, let yourself ask this. We are not always sure how to know the answer to this question. This takes listening to ourselves and our lives honestly and clearly. Here are a few more notes on pushes and pulls that will help you clarify what you are feeling.

Being pulled often includes the sensation of popping out of bed in the morning ready to embrace the day, or losing track of time while you're actively engaged in a project you love. A pull can be felt in any activity or any moment in your life: spending time with someone, collaborating on a project, reading a book, going to the gym, thinking about something you see while traveling, organizing your house, writing, taking a class, resolving a computer problem, and so on. Any of these and other things may be a pull for you. You feel yourself energized and flowing with your natural rhythm when you are feeling a pull, feeling yourself pulled toward.

A push is different, and there are different signals when you are having the feeling of pushing against. Pushes may even be expressed via physical signals. You may do something or be involved in something that feels in your body like a push: you may feel tight or painful energy in your stomach, shoulders, back, or wherever you hold tension. Or you may feel a push emotionally rather than physically. For example, you may feel guilty, lazy, angry, resentful, or fatigued.

Note: Of course you don't have to start to notice, let alone work through, all your pushes and pulls as these arise. Sometimes you are just too busy, or tired, or are not feeling great and cannot see your pushes and pulls clearly.

When you are ready, then go ahead and give thought to your pushes and your pulls. Do this when you feel like doing so, when you have the energy, when you are inspired to.

Pulls may seem to you to be the few sweet moments of distraction in your life, moments that you cherish or find good in some way, maybe moments that make you feel like you are getting away with something.

You might think that the pulls you feel are wrong, that these are just you goofing off, taking the easy way out. And you might think that the pushes you feel are what make you a good person, are what you "should" do, or are what make you "do the right thing."

And you might even feel that doing what you are pushing against will actually get you to where you want to go, or at least where you believe you should go.

But where are you going if you are leaving your authentic self behind? You aren't going anywhere without your authentic self, as the compromised self is not you. Where the compromised self goes is not where you go, not really. You will see this as you become more aware of your true, your authentic, self.

Your power, traction,
and peace
arise from being
one with your authentic self.

Listen to your pushes
so you know what is going on.

Your authentic self
will tell you
when you feel
you cannot be authentic.

So don't miss the
opportunity to
listen to your pushes.

And then be sure you
look for your pulls.

Step 1
SEEING MY
PUSHES/PULLS EXERCISE

It is now time to focus your awareness to how you move, flow, your energy. This exercise addresses exactly this. To do this exercise, take out your journal. Select two pages of your journal, one right after the other. At the top of one of the pages, write PUSHING AGAINST. At the top of the other page, write BEING PULLED TOWARD.

You will want to record your pushes and pulls at the end of the day, or whenever you have time to reflect on your day. I suggest you work with what we will call your PUSHES/PULLS until you have a strong sense of who you are and where your pulls get stopped by pushes.

You may want to write down your PUSHES/PULLS for a few days or a week until you feel you have enough data to work with. Recording your PUSHES/PULLS may even become a valuable lifelong habit. The more PUSHES/PULLS you have written down, the more data you will have to work with.

TWO THINGS TO KEEP IN MIND WHILE YOU ARE RECORDING YOUR PUSHES/PULLS

(1) The first is to do this exercise without judgment. You are the scribe recording the flow of your energy. There is nothing you have to do with the information you record in this step, Step 1. You are just recording what you are feeling. You will work with this data you are gathering in the next several steps.

(2) The second thing to keep in mind is that you want to be as specific as possible when you record your PUSHES/PULLS, as if you are experiencing these in the moment. The more specific you are, the clearer the information you will receive from your PUSHES/PULLS.

RESISTING THE FLOW IS PUSHING

When you feel yourself resisting something, or when you have the feeling of pushing against, make a note of it. Write this down in your journal. You will know this pushing against feeling because this feeling is much like what you would feel if you were trying to swim against a current, against a flow.

You may experience the sense of a pit in your stomach or a tightness in your chest. When you get this feeling, write down what you were doing or thinking about when this feeling came over you. Perhaps someone said something to you, or maybe you were working on a project you disliked, or maybe you felt awkward in a particular social situation.

List these on the page of your journal with the words PUSHING AGAINST at the top. At the end of the day, highlight your strongest of the day. Do this for each day you engage in this first step and this Step 1 Exercise.

Your strongest pushes are the easiest to get information from. Later in this book, when you get to STEP 4: UNDERSTANDING YOUR RESISTANCE, these are the pushes you will want to work with first.

THE OPPOSITE OF PUSHING IS BEING PULLED TOWARD, GOING WITH THE FLOW....

When you feel your energy calling you forth, when you find yourself gravitating to something, make a note of this on the page of your journal with the heading, BEING PULLED.

The activity you make a note about can be almost anything. This can be a conversation you were engaged in, a request someone made of you, a comment someone made, a call from a client, an interaction with your child, a commercial you saw on television. This can even be something you read on the Internet, or a certain food item you saw when grocery shopping, etc. Nothing is too trivial.

Put all that pulls you on this list of pulls. Just like the pushes, a pull can be something you were doing or even just a thought you were thinking. Again, each evening make a note of, and highlight with a star or check mark, your strongest pull of the day. Do this each day you work on this Step 1 Exercise. A few pages from now, when you get to STEP 2: REVEALING YOUR VALUES, it will be easiest to gather information from your strongest pulls.

You are writing down your PUSHES/PULLS as a response to what you are experiencing, feeling. Did you feel your energy being pulled toward or did you feel your energy pushing against? As you won't be able to write down all the pushes and pulls you experience throughout any one day, write down the ones that hold the most energy for you, highlight your strongest push and your strongest pull for each day you are recording these.

Step One
Seeing My Pushes/Pulls
Exercise Chart

Step 1
Seeing My Pushes/Pulls
Exercise

My Pushes

____

____

____

____

____

My Pulls

____

____

____

____

____

Some examples of pushes and pulls from the SEEING MY PUSHES/PULLS EXERCISE

PUSHING AGAINST
(resisting the flow)

1. Hearing my mom call and ask me about the upcoming holiday dinner.
2. Hearing my husband criticize the outfit I am wearing.
3. Having to drive my son to baseball practice.
4. Realizing I forgot to pay the insurance bill.
5. Receiving the announcement for the class reunion.
6. Waiting in line to check into my hotel.
7. Agreeing to meet with my friend for coffee.
8. Seeing the drip irrigation isn't working.
9. Noticing when the conversation at the party turned to politics.
10. Having my supervisor pile more work on my desk.

BEING PULLED TOWARD
(going with the flow)

1. Making dinner tonight while listening to music.
2. Having a conversation with my friend about our upcoming bike trip.
3. Looking over the seed catalog that came in the mail.
4. Making a new dish for my family.
5. Preparing for my presentation at work.
6. Clearing out the pantry.
7. Putting a bid on a new piece of property.
8. Teaching my science class.
9. Going on my morning walk.
10. Collaborating on a new business project.

WHY DO WE RESIST OUR LIVES?

What we feel resistance to can tell us a lot about ourselves. This resisting is not an unusual behavior. In fact it is quite common.

Go to your journal and look at your own list of pushes. One of the first words that typically pop to the surface when listing pushes is the word "should." By should I mean both "should" and "should not" as these are both shoulds. You either *shouldn't be* feeling what you are feeling or you *should* feel differently.

When you feel a should and respond to it with stress, tension, pressure, or anger, or resistance of another form, this is a clue. Any resistance you feel, no matter what form this resistance takes, is the first clue that you are resisting, even abandoning, your authentic self.

For example, you might say to yourself things like this:

> I shouldn't feel frustrated when my mom calls to talk about the holiday dinner.
> I shouldn't care that my husband criticizes my outfit.
> I should want to drive my son to baseball.
> I should have paid the insurance bill on time.
> I should want to go to the class reunion.
> I shouldn't complain about waiting in line at the hotel.
> I should want to meet my friend for coffee.
> I should make sure the drip irrigation is working.
> I should be comfortable talking about politics.
> I shouldn't complain about the extra work.

Each of the above is an example of a push.

There is more to say about pushes, which I will do later in this book, when we get to Step 4: UNDERSTANDING YOUR RESISTANCE. For now, note that:

We are often quite hesitant to admit to or write down our pushes, because we believe we shouldn't be feeling what we're feeling. You might notice that the first place your thoughts go is:

"It's my fault, I'm doing something wrong here."

These judgments we have about ourselves are what cause us to feel constriction in our flow. Remember that the flow itself does not constrict, it is only our perception that the flow is constricting that we are responding to.

As we move forward through these 5 Steps to your authentic self and life, you will come to understand that there is wisdom in your resistance. You will find valuable information about your authentic self in your pushes.

So at this point in the process, don't be too quick to judge your pushes and pulls; don't be too ready to say what is good or bad, right or wrong. Your authentic self is good, and that is that. However, sometimes it takes a little unraveling to fully grasp this concept. Be patient with yourself while you work the 5 Steps in this book. Each time you do these steps you will learn more about yourself.

REFLECTIONS ON THE SEEING MY PUSHES/PULLS EXERCISE

When doing the SEEING MY PUSHES/PULLS EXERCISE that is part of Step 1, you may find something interesting taking place, something interesting or perplexing perhaps. At times, you may feel that you are experiencing a push and a pull simultaneously. This is quite common, especially in the early stages of this process.

What is happening is that the thoughts are coming in, either so vaguely or so quickly, that you are unable to separate them. So these thoughts collapse in on one another and blur together.

By slowing down and slowing down your thinking, you will be able to recognize when a pull (something your authentic self is pulling you to) drifts into a push (something your authentic self is pushing against in some way) and vice versa. When telling yourself you are feeling pushed and or pulled, just be as specific as you can with yourself. Over time you will be more and more able to separate these feelings.

Do not worry if you are uncertain about which is a push for you and which is a pull. Just write everything down on the two lists you have in your journal, the PUSHING AGAINST list and the PULLING TOWARD list. Do this according to the above SEEING MY PUSHES/PULLS EXERCISE, just listing things where you think they best fit. No need to make this complicated or worrisome. This exercise is about becoming more and more aware of yourself and of your energy. You are simply starting to more carefully develop your self awareness muscle and to become more familiar with your authentic self.

ALSO NOTE

You may be surprised at what a push is for you and at what a pull is for you. For example, you may think spending time alone with your spouse would be a pull and then find out that most of the time this is a push for you.

Again, don't judge – don't judge yourself because being with your spouse may feel like a push. This is all just information at this point. Do this exercise at your own pace.

You can't get any of this wrong. Sometimes we are on some level afraid of this sort of information and think we have to change something in our lives because we find a push. Yet none of this is so simple. Resist the temptation to try and figure out any solutions at this point or to feel you have to make any abrupt changes in your life. Just collect information about yourself and about what feels to be a push or a pull to you.

You are
like a scribe,
gathering information
for
further study.

I have explained here that the SEEING MY PUSHES/PULLS EXERCISE is a very simple exercise. And yet this exercise can also seem complex. The exercise itself is simple but we humans are very complex. Our lives are filled with both inspiration and conflicting thoughts throughout the day, most every day. You may already be noticing this on a daily basis, or you may sense this when you reflect on your lists of pushes and pulls once you've written them down.

Do not be concerned about this mix of simplicity and complexity. Real personal growth involves both.

If we are really listening to ourselves, our greatest inner conflicts can provide us the greatest path to clarity.

There are many occasions when we feel we should act certain ways and do certain things whether or not we truly want to be these ways and do these things. You may hear yourself saying, "Well there are things I have to do, I don't have a choice."

Yes and no. Maybe you have more choice in the matter than you are initially seeing. The freedom you are looking for does not necessarily mean changing the outer circumstances in your life, although sometimes it does. A life full of the sort of energy you feel when being pushed is a life that leaves little room for the energy you feel when you are drawn to your pulls. Being pressured by too many pushes leaves little room for you to express and be what you are being pulled to express and be.

It may be easier to notice one of your pushes or pulls when you are taking action, when you are in the middle of doing something. But you may also notice a push and or a pull as simply a form of thought. Or the thought you are feeling pushed or pulled by may come to you while doing something else not related to this thought.

For example, you may feel a pull while sipping on a cup of tea after a long day and then a thought pops in about the work left behind at the office and you find yourself in the middle of a push. The more you do the SEEING MY PUSHES/PULLS EXERCISE, the more aware of your self you will become. With ongoing use of this simple exercise, you will eventually have access to what is really going on within you.

You will discover who you are and who you are not.

You will begin to recognize yourself in your pulls, in what you feel truly pulled toward, truly interested in, truly desiring of.

If a situation or a thought pulls you, this is because you recognize yourself, the essence of who you are, in that situation or thought. This is the feeling of coming home to yourself. Over time, your pulls will become very familiar to you. And then when you feel a push you will know something is off. You will feel the times when you are turning away from your authentic self, either through your actions or through your thoughts.

Once you become aware of the feeling, the energy, of your pushes and of your pulls, you will never again have to travel very far from your authentic self. When you feel yourself pushed and drifting away from your true self, you will know the choices you can make to come back.

DO NOT BE AFRAID OF SEEING YOUR SELF

Looking honestly at yourself and at your feelings will not harm you. Ultimately, once you get used to looking at and being honest with yourself, you are not going to find anything within your true self that you do not love. The process of living a happy life is a lifetime journey: the journey of revealing more and more of the pure goodness and magnificence that you are.

Remember that in Step 1 there is nothing for you to do with or about your push/pulls. You are just gathering data for further study. You are just getting to see these pushes and pulls, and to list them so you can remember them and use them later.

You will find that your emotions are signs of many of your pushes and pulls. Be aware of your emotions and know that every emotion has a beginning, a middle, and an end. Think of your emotions as being like waves. These waves may have gentle rolling motions or more powerful cresting actions.

Regardless of the intensity of these waves, you will notice the energy beginning to form and then to peak and then to begin to recede. The same wave motion is true for your emotions. If you are feeling anger, this anger may come upon you as a sudden burst of energy or it may have been simmering for awhile. Either way, the intensity of this anger does not stay level. Like a wave it will build, crest and recede.

So follow the waves of your emotions, see how they build, crest, and recede. See what these emotions tell you you are feeling, and what these emotions are telling you about your pushes and pulls. You'll write down your push/pulls at the time that is best for you.

You may find it easier to jot down your pushes close to the heat of the moment so these are fresh for you. Or you may want any related emotion to simmer down so you can get some distance on it first. Make notes on your pushes, and on your pulls, when it works for you to write these.

This work is not about snuffing out your emotions prematurely to try to feel better as quickly as possible. You will feel better soon enough. Your emotions contain a wealth of information. You want to mine as much of this information as possible while you are working this 5 step process.

By taking the time to look deeply into your push/pulls now, you will actually quicken the process of shifting your energy in the future. The more you know how your energy naturally likes to flow, the more masterful you will be in directing it.

The simple but central Step 1 SEEING MY PUSHES/PULLS EXERCISE will also be used in the next steps, Steps 2 through 5, to support you in living the gift that you are. These steps are part of the process of learning to fully participate in the giving and receiving flow of life. It is time now to reveal your authentic self....

**Noticing how you
use and flow your energy
is the first step in coming into
alignment with your true self,
with your most authentic self.**

If you feel you have become detached from your authentic self, learn to know your pushes and pulls. Your pushes and pulls are beacons of light guiding you to your true self. This is a wonderful journey and the path is well lit once you become adept at discerning your pushes and pulls.

21
Step Two:
Revealing Your Values

STEP 2: REVEALING YOUR VALUES is the second step in the process of *living an authentically happy life*. This step is about looking deep inside, seeing what you are really about. This is about clarifying for yourself what you truly value, what is most important to you, what you love.

Being clear about your own particular set of values is knowing yourself and knowing what makes you unique. When you truly know yourself, the cloud of confusion lifts and you feel your confidence come pouring in.

You may be asking what your true values are and how you can know. This is not always easy to know. After all, we have values, we think we know what our values are, however many of our values are defined by the world around us, outside us.

These may or may not be our true values. In fact, if something is not a real value for you, it is not really a value of your own. It may be someone else's value. Or it may be a belief that something should be one of your values, but it is not one of your own personal values.

KNOW YOUR OWN VALUES

Look around, there are so many different values to identify with. You probably could look at a list of hundreds of common values and agree that many of them are important. Perhaps you would say that all the values listed are important. But look again. You will see that there are some values that hold more energy for you than other values do. Ask yourself, "What is most important to me, what three or four things do I value most?" Give yourself some time to name these values, your own personal values. You will find that you do prioritize your values. You will see that you live your life according to your values. Or at least you want to – on some deep level your authentic self wants to.

Your authentic self wants to live your daily life according to your own primary values. Your values show in the way you want to give and the way you want to receive time, energy, resources, love, whatever you value. Your values show in what affects your decisions and choices. Where you are not acting according to your own values, you feel this, you know this on some level.

Most of the time, we not only give according to our values, but we receive according to these values as well. For example, if you value being respected, you value respecting others. If you value beauty, you probably enjoy creating beauty as well as absorbing the beauty others have created. If you value honesty, you value being honest as well as others being honest with you. Your values are areas of your life where you place a lot of your focus and attention, or perhaps a lot of your emotional energy.

Now, some readers may be saying, "I am not sure I live according to my values. But if I do, I am not sure I both give and receive according to my values. How can I know? How can I know what my truest values are?" Let's dig in deeper here to know more about personal values.

WHAT IS A PERSONAL VALUE?

We live our daily lives, frequently too busy to focus on or define clearly all of our values. We know in general that a value is a philosophy that guides us, even when we are not consciously aware this guidance is taking place. We take many of our values in from our societies, our families, our communities, our religions, and sometimes our professions as well. Values are most definitely valuable. They give purpose and meaning to our lives and behaviors. We hear famous people report that they are guided by their strong personal values. Just as many successful people we hear about in the media have a strong sense of purpose, so do you.

Knowing your values allows you to feel purpose in what you do, think, say and feel. Each and every one of us follows the guidance of our own values when we make choices and decisions about our lives and our behaviors.

Among the many values we see at work within and around us are values such as those listed below. There are so many values out there, only a few are listed here as examples. Of course we do not all share all of these values, or possibly do not share any of these values. Still, each of us has our own set of personal values that may include some of these common personal values:

EXAMPLES OF PERSONAL VALUES

Accomplishment, adventure, beauty, calm, charity, cleanliness, commitment, community, competence, connection, cooperation, creativity, depth, discipline, efficiency, fairness, family, freedom, friendship, fun, generosity, harmony, health, honor, honesty, independence, innovation, integrity, intelligence, inspiration, justice, kindness, leadership, love, loyalty, order, peace, perfection, perseverance, playfulness, privacy, productivity, prosperity, punctuality, purpose, reliability, respect, safety, security, self-care, self-reliance, sensitivity, simplicity, significance, spirituality, stability, strength, teamwork, tolerance, tradition, trust, truth, unity.

So how do you name your own personal values? How do you choose which values are yours? The REVEALING MY VALUES EXERCISE here in Step 2 will help you reveal to yourself what you truly value and what matters most to you in your life.

Step 2
REVEALING MY VALUES EXERCISE

If you were asked to write a list of your values, you might be tempted to write down what you believe you should value. This is natural, as many of us are told throughout our lives what we are supposed to believe is important, supposed to believe is valuable. However your own personal values are not necessarily what others have told you you should value.

In this exercise, you will be seeking to notice and name your own personal values even if these values are not exactly what the outside world tells you you should value. You started listing your pushes and pulls in Step 1: BECOMING AWARE where you did the SEEING MY PUSHES/PULLS EXERCISE.

Now you can use these pushes and pulls you listed to take you to the next level. You are ready to see the theme of your values. As your values reflect who you are, you are ready to find your authentic self in these values, when these values are authentic.

You can get an honest portrayal of your values by scanning your list of pulls. When you are experiencing PULLs, when you are drawn to, pulled to, activities and behaviors, you are acting on and living your values. Focus on the idea that when you are living your values you feel yourself being pulled. You are aligned with your true self, going with the flow of your life and of all life. And this feels good. This feels right.

Now take a moment and go back to the pulls you have highlighted in your journal. Rewrite these pulls on a new journal page, under the heading MY VALUES. Now, next to each pull on your pulls list, describe the value you are living or the value you imagine yourself living when you experience this pull. You may have more than one value for each pull.

Once you have compiled your list of values this way, scan the list and see if you can begin to get a feel for who you are. Feel the energy of your values and how grounding it feels to admit the truth of who you are. The combination of your values will be unique to you. You will want to keep adding and articulating these values until you have a good sense of what these mean to you.

Examples of Values
Taken from Pulls Listed for the
REVEALING MY VALUES EXERCISE

1. Pull - Signing up for a writing class.
   Values:
   Self expression, creativity, being focused, clarity, learning.

2. Pull - Visiting the dogs at the animal shelter.
   Values:
   Life, compassion, love, community, play, helping.

3. Pull - Attending the meditation class.
   Values:
   Peace, connection, community, silence, relaxation.

4. Pull - Making homemade pizza on the grill.
   Values:
   Creativity, being outdoors, nurturing, family.

5. Pull - Shopping spree I went on with my niece.
   Values:
   Playfulness, connection, family, fashion, fun.

6. Pull - Working on my water color painting.
   Values:
   Beauty, creative expression, sensitivity, focus, nature, productivity.

7. Pull - Preparing for our backpacking trip.
   Values:
   Organization, adventure, self-reliance, strength, connection, friendship, health.

8. Pull - Completing the audit at work.
   Values:
   Productivity, completion, accomplishment, accountability.

9. Pull – Working on the committee for fundraising.
   Values:
   Leadership, teamwork, fun, community, collaboration.

10. Pull – Opening up my investment account.
   Values:
   Independence, financial security, freedom, planning.

Step Two
Revealing My Values
Exercise Chart

Step 2
Revealing My Values
Exercise

My Pulls	My Values

EXPLORING VALUES

You are what you truly value, what is most important to you. What you truly value is what you love. When your thoughts, words and actions are aligned with what you truly value, what you truly love, you feel yourself being pulled. When you go with your own pulls, you are harmonizing with your own values and with the greater flow of life. On the other hand, when you go against what you truly value, you have the feeling of pushing against. This pushing against sensation may be a subtle feeling, or it may make itself known to you loud and clear.

Don't miss the opportunity to notice and receive this communication. The more you allow yourself to feel the difference between expressing your own values and withholding your own values, the more you know yourself. It is that simple.

Take a moment to reflect on your list of values. Even if the words for your values are the same as another person's words, what those values mean to you are specific to you. You may not even be able to describe what they mean to you, it may just be a feeling, a knowing you have. See if you can start to detect a theme in your values.

Maybe you prefer intimate relationships with your friends, family and co-workers. Or you may enjoy expanding your energy in a wider range, interacting with many people at once. You may notice you prefer going deep inside yourself with your energy, or wide out into the world with your energy. Or perhaps you prefer a combination of these directions for your energy, each direction of your energy depending upon the particular activity you are involved in. You may also detect a theme in the rhythm of your energy; precise, intense, general, casual or relaxed.

There is no right way to be. And if you weren't this way you would be another way, you would use your own particular energy in your own particular way.

For example, even though two people may have the desire to

invest in commercial real estate, they may be doing it based on very different values. One person may value the excitement, adventure, fun, and community aspect of investing in real estate. And another may do it because he or she values security and stability. You may say how could that be possible? How could they both desire real estate investing and yet have such apparently conflicting values? As I have said, this process is very personal to you and you don't have to explain yourself to another.

The only
values you have to be
aligned with
are your own.

And the only person
that needs
to understand
these values you have
is
you.

The person who values excitement, adventure, fun, and community may say, "But I also value stability and security." Yes, that may be true, but maybe not to the same degree or defined the same way as it is by the other person. Everyone differs in terms of values. You differ from even the persons you are closest to.

There are always differences, personal differences, although sometimes these are minor. Always know that your own particular energy is looking for something entirely your own. As you become more aware of yourself, your authentic self, you will notice how your values are present in all the activities you enjoy pursuing.

Be sure to look for any ways any shoulds are telling you what to value. If you watch for times you are thinking you "should" be or think a certain way, you will be able to see when your own personal values are being withheld.

Let's say you value time by yourself. You are home by yourself gardening, experiencing a wonderful pull while doing this. Then someone comes to your house and says, "What's wrong with you? You are so boring. Let's go out for some excitement." If you say yes to this but you don't really want to go, you'll have the feeling of selling out on yourself – and you will experience a push.

THIS IS WHO I AM

By reviewing your values, you will notice you put more weight on some values than on others. You can't and wouldn't want to put equal value on everything. Some of your values are more important to you than others. When you align your life with your true values, you are putting a stake in the ground and declaring: This is who I am.

There is a special peace that washes over you when you recognize yourself in your values. From this place of clarity you stop fighting against others, stop trying to convince them of your worthiness. And you drop your defensiveness. You turn within and recognize your wholeness. You realize you can stop working so hard to get others to agree with you.

One of the biggest conflicts we have with others is trying to convince them our values are right while their values are wrong. However, there is no "right" way to be. There is no "right" set of values. If we didn't have the values we have, we would have other values.

As I said earlier, we are each individualized expressions of Spirit contributing to the whole. And we each have a unique contribution to make to the whole. We actually compliment each other when we are not entangled in our pushing against (diminishing) thoughts.

We're not cut out of a cookie cutter mold, although often we act as if we are or wish we were. This stance comes from a misunderstanding: the misunderstanding that says another person can take away from us what we value. But he or she can't. Agreement from others is not what makes you whole. Claiming your own values brings you to your self, to your wholeness. You begin to unify with yourself.

ONE OF THE MOST VALUABLE THINGS YOU CAN DO

One of the most valuable things you can do in this lifetime is to take the time to identify and realize what you value.

**Knowing your
true values
gives you
the freedom
to be
your authentic self
and to live a
life of integrity,
an authentic life.**

You will feel the beauty and ease of aligning with yourself. The synergies of your values are what make you unique.

And, there are going to be differences in people's own personal values. There are also going to be different combinations of values held by people. This is because each one of us is our own particular authentic self who wants to live our own particular authentic life.

You will see that as you continue to clarify and define your own values, to define for yourself what your own combination of your own personal values is, no one else will have exactly your set of values with your own interpretation of your values. There is not another person on the planet that has precisely your combination of values. You see, no one but you is your own authentic self.

WHEN YOU FEEL SOME OF YOUR VALUES CONTRADICT

Also note: As you put together your list of values, some of your values may appear to contradict one another. For example, you might ask yourself, "How can I love time alone so very much and still love to connect with others?"

Yet this set of values can make complete sense. The degrees of alone time and connecting time you value will be unique to you. There are an infinite number of combinations of values you can have, each combination of values weighted specifically by you.

Until you can recognize and list enough of your own personal values to form what is uniquely your own list, there is still more to discover about yourself. You don't want to stop with something like, "I value creativity and adventure." Although this can cover a broad spectrum, you are more than this.

What makes you unique is your own specific combination of specific values.

ACKNOWLEDGE YOUR OWN VALUES

Acknowledging your own set of your own true values allows you to tune into your personal energy, your own personal frequency. When you know what you value, your brain's receptors start clearly picking up what is yours to do, to be, to express, and what is not yours to do, to be, to express. When you know what you value, you have the sense of being grounded, of being clear enough to live from your values.

As you do the Step 2: REVEALING MY VALUES EXERCISE that I have provided on the preceding pages, you may start to notice that your strongest values relate to what you love to give and to receive. If a strong value of yours is inspiration, chances are you love to inspire and you love to be inspired.

When you are allowing yourself to be what you are, you can feel the energy of being in the giving and receiving flow. Most if not all of us love to give on some level, in some way. It is in our nature to give. If we are not giving, something is obstructing our flow.

We will further discuss this matter of blocking your flow in Step 4: UNDERSTANDING YOUR RESISTANCE. For now, keep in mind that our deepest desire is to live our strongest values. And one of our biggest fears is that we will not be able to live those values. We are often afraid that we will have to sell out on ourselves, that we will have to be someone other than who we truly are just to fit in, to be accepted, or to survive.

You will feel a deep sense of peace and satisfaction when you realize that you do not have to value or act like you value what you do not value. You do not have to be someone you are not. You do not have to be anyone or anything other than who you are. Who you are is enough for one lifetime.

YOU CANNOT IMPROVE ON THE PERFECTION THAT IS YOU

I used to be a champion of self improvement. I believed that if I just berated myself enough, fixed what was wrong and worked harder, all my dreams would come true. I eventually found that this was not the case.

When you understand the truth of who you are, you discover that self improvement is a myth. The self improvement model is usually focused on what is wrong and then attempts to come up with solutions to fix the problem.

This approach doesn't work because the persons and organizations giving advice on how to improve are basing this on their own values and their own expressions of their own values. They are saying, "just do what I do or be like me and your life will work so much better." While their intentions may be good, their underlying theme is saying, "My way is right and yours does not work. I'm right and you're wrong." Yet, following someone else's path to fulfillment or even self improvement does not lead you to your own self, nor to your own authentically happy life.

What can improve is the quality of your life. This quality of your life doesn't improve because you fix something about yourself, something that you are told is broken. Rather, this quality of your life improves because you release your compromised self. You let go of the persona you thought you had to be to survive in the world.

When you release who you are not, the beauty of who you are shines through. The quality of your life improves because you are no longer withholding your authentic self. You are free to be your true self, and you can't improve on this perfection that you already are. As you will see in Step 4, your part is to release the misunderstandings and misperceptions about yourself that you are carrying around.

There is nothing you need to add to or improve about yourself, but there is plenty you can release and break free of. All you need to do to be the real you is to …

release the misperceptions
you have inherited
or picked up along the way
and then

reveal the
actual values and true beauty
that lie within you.

Your desires will guide you in the most effective and best way for you to live your values. Desires are the expression of your values. Following your true desires is how you share your highest most beautiful self with the world. In the next step, Step 3, you will begin to recognize the desires that are calling you to be your authentic self.

22
Step Three: Recognizing Your Desires

STEP 3: RECOGNIZING YOUR DESIRES is the third step in living your authentic life. So many of us either are not aware of what we truly desire, or believe we do not deserve to make what we truly desire front and center in our lives.

There can be good reasons for your not knowing or expressing your truest desires. Many of us have been taught to look to the world around us for direction on what to desire and what to do.

As you begin to explore your desires, it is important to understand the difference between your values and your desires.

Your values are
the timeless,
the eternal,
part of you.

You can think of your values as the absolute, the invisible behind the visible. Some may call the body of your true values your God self or your higher self. I prefer to call this ***your authentic self***. This describes the essence, the purity, of what you are.

TRY THE I AM PROCESS

When you place the words "I am" in front of one of your values, you can feel yourself resonating with what is true for you. Try this I AM process by placing this I AM in front of each of your own values. For example: *I am* love, *I am* adventure, *I am* fun, *I am* creative, *I am* beauty, *I am* truth, *I am* lightness, I *am* order. *I am* secure. The essence of what you are gets released into the world when you follow the desires of your heart.

Values can be expressed throughout life, sometimes changing in expression, sometimes staying the same. When you were younger, your value of creativity may have been expressed by building sandcastles. And as you grew older, that value may have been expressed by designing a computer program. Or through the years, your value of connection may have been expressed through your relationships, with your best friends, spouses, children, co-workers, or your community.

Being in touch with your truest values, the process you started working on in Step 2, helps you come to your true desires.

Your desires are
how you choose to
express and live your values.

YOUR DESIRES WILL PULL YOU

Your desires, your true desires, pull you. They pull you forward into the giving and receiving flow of life. You can think of your values as what you are, and of your desires as what you do as an expression of what you are. Your desires are how you express your values, and how you shape and mold your expression of your values. For example, eating raw food or cycling may be how you shape your value of health.

This is about how you take the invisible part of you, your values, and live these out on the physical plane. Your values may seem to be similar to another person's values, but how *you* express *your* values, *your* desires, may not look at all like the way someone else chooses to live his or her values.

Just like giving and receiving are not one sided transactions, so it is with your desires. For example, if you have the desire to buy organic food, there are people who have the desire to sell it to you. The ultimate giving and receiving flow of all life is always in balance. Just let yourself be aware of this.

What you desire
is longing
to be
lived through you.

WHAT YOU TRULY DESIRE

Let me say this again: What you truly desire for yourself is longing to be lived through you. To be happy, you will want to listen to yourself. You will want to get in touch with what you truly desire. And yet even though I say this, that you will want to listen to yourself to know your desires:

You already know
what you truly desire.

You may have grown numb to your desires, protecting yourself from the disappointment of not being allowed to live them. But if you listen, your desires are there, right there inside you, awaiting your expression. Sometimes, too often, we can be hesitant to tune in and listen to our truest desires. We tend to do this when we fear that following our truest desires will take us away from the people we love, or that we will lose what we value if we act on our deepest desires. Or maybe we are afraid that if we act on these desires, if we truly start thinking for ourselves, people will think we are self-centered.

When you hear the word "desire" you may say to yourself, "well if everyone followed his or her desires, our society would fall apart. People would be stealing, they would quit their jobs, lay around all day, drink too much, eat too much, etc." This fear comes to us only when we are unfamiliar with the flow and the true nature of people.

Destructive behaviors do not come out of people being authentic with themselves. Destructive behaviors come out of people resisting the flow and feeling cut off and separate from life. People engaged in destructive behaviors are feeling powerless and looking for a way to experience more relief and less pain.

LOOK CLOSELY

False desires are not authentic desires. False desires don't really satisfy you for long. False desires sometimes seem like true desires at the outset. And these false desires can diminish your resistance for awhile: you may not realize you are pushing against the flow (your flow, your true self) while you act on these false desires. These false desires may even feel like pulls for a while, but they are not really pulls.

Look closely at
your desires
to know whether
they are false desires
or are
your very own
authentic desires.

When a desire is a false desire, you will know this. You will know how you truly feel about this desire. And you will know when your true desire is not being acted on, when instead you are acting on a false desire. But don't worry. There is no way you can get this wrong.

For example, by following what appears to be a true desire, when it isn't really a true desire of your own, the truth about this desire will be revealed. Indeed, what may have begun as a pull for you may cross over to become a push for you as you travel further down the path.

When my clients are not clear on whether something is a true or a false desire, I encourage them to follow the energy because the truth will be revealed.

And know that sometimes desires change. The energy of a desire will either grow stronger or this energy will begin to dissipate. Over time, if it turns out the desire is a false desire, the feeling of dissatisfaction will grow. Soon the truth about the desire you are acting on reveals itself: as you continue to follow this desire you will feel the sensation of a push. This is a sign that the false desire is not really what your heart is longing to be, to do, to live (at least not right now). There is a better more satisfying choice for you to make.

We want to live, express and share our true selves with the world. No one enjoys feeling less than who he or she is. This less than feeling is like gasping for air, trying to catch your breath. People will do just about anything to feel some relief. But this relief is not authentic relief. Your own personal evolution goes way beyond just surviving.

You don't have to take my word for it. Practice living with the 5 Steps I share in this book. When you then recognize you are in the flow, bring your awareness to the desires you are following. Notice that when you say yes to your authentic self, people around you also benefit.

When we live from our inauthentic, compromised, "should" selves, very often we are filled with frustration, tension, maybe even resentment, maybe even anger. Yet as we begin to move toward our authentic selves, our energy softens and we end up feeling more compassion for ourselves and others. The more time we spend being aware of the true values that we hold, the more we have to share with others.

We realize our values are not finite. We allow ourselves to be filled with a knowing of the truth of who we are. There is more of us available to share. Our cup runneth over.

We grow and expand
through
the following of
our true desires...

...and the living of
our true values.

If you are feeling separate from the flow, experiencing resistance from within either by judging yourself or others, what I am sharing about true desires here may not make sense at first. I can understand that you may be thinking that if you claim more for yourself, there will be less for others.

But I promise you, this process doesn't work that way because life doesn't work that way. By working with these 5 Steps, you will discover what I am saying for yourself:

Knowing and living
your truest desires
for yourself
is not selfish.

YOUR DESIRES ARE NOT RANDOM

If you tune in and listen, you will realize that the desires in your heart are very customized and unique to you. These are the expression of your values, of what is most important to you. Even if you have been ignoring your true desires, they haven't gone anywhere.

These desires, these yearnings within your soul, want to be brought out into the world and they want to be lived through you. You are the person perfectly designed to fulfill the desires you are receiving.

Your desires form the roadmap that connects you to your truest, most authentic, self. You are pulled by your desires into the current of your life and you feel this pull. Your own desires are not random; rather they are very personal and specific to you. When you follow a true desire, you are catching the wave that wants to happen. It is the direct path into your flow. Do not be concerned if this makes only some sense to you at this time. You will find that the more you go over this material and use your personal data from your push/pulls, the more all this will speak to you.

As you feel your pushes and pulls throughout the day, you can tell when you are following your desires, being pulled toward what you truly desire to be and to do. And, you will also notice when you feel powerless to be who you are, when you are pushing against being your authentic self. This is a moment to moment awareness. We go in and out of our pushes and pulls throughout the day.

**The measurement of
living a happy life
is to be able to
stay in the
giving and receiving flow
for longer and longer
periods of time:**

**in the flow as
your authentic self.**

THERE IS A LIGHT WITHIN YOU

Even if you have been feeling that unpleasant pushing against sensation for a long time, been swimming against the current for years, there is a light within you that has not gone out.

This light, this yearning within your soul, wants to be brought out and shared with the world. If there weren't desires within you wanting to be birthed and expressed, you wouldn't feel any push-type resistance. You wouldn't feel when you were not being your authentic self.

Always remember that your truest desires are an expression of your values.

And your values are your authentic self.

Again, I want to say that living as your authentic self is a process that unfolds moment by moment. Take your time to find your light, and to allow your self and your life to fully shine. As you feel your pushes and pulls throughout the day, you can tell when you are following your inner light and when you are attempting to snuff it out. Every step of the way, giving yourself permission to follow your inner light will be your path to your authentic self.

Step 3
RECOGNIZING MY DESIRES EXERCISE

When you are following your inner desires, you feel yourself being pulled to do so. Desires are an energy calling you forth. And when you say yes to your truest desires, you can feel your energy being pulled into the flow of life. Each time you experience a pull, this is an indication you are pulled to say yes to a true desire. You can make this choice.

Look at your desires and ask yourself some questions, "Why is this desire such a strong pull for me? What about this desire do I resonate with? What values of mine does this desire express?"

Copy the list of your own values, the list that you came up with during the Step 2: REVEALING MY VALUES EXERCISE. List these values on another page of your journal, a new page now. Review the values you have on this list and notice the connection between your values and your desires. Notice how your desires are an expression of your values.

Now list your pulls for each of the values you have listed. You can go back to your Steps 1 and 2 for these. Remember, you used your list of pulls (the ones you wrote in Step 1) to list your values (in Step 2). So you have used your lists to see how your pulls reveal your values.

Your pulls which reflect your values also reflect your true desires. Therefore your pulls can lead you right into the flow of living as your authentic self.

So now, for this exercise, go to the list of your values you have on this new page of your journal. Next to each value, list some of your desires, desires that relate to that value. Where you do not see a value that fuels a particular desire, write the desire down anyway. Then think of a value the desire is expressing.

For example, if you value fun, just write that down as the value behind a desire to have fun by doing something in particular. There is more than one door to your authentic self. You can access information about your authentic self through your values and desires. (And as you will see in Step 4, also through your resistance.)

Step Three
Recognizing My Desires
Exercise Chart

Step 3
Recognizing My Desires
Exercise

My Pulls	My Values	My Desires
________	________	________
________	________	________
________	________	________
________	________	________
________	________	________
________	________	________
________	________	________
________	________	________
________	________	________
________	________	________
________	________	________
________	________	________

Examples of Expressions of Values for the RECOGNIZING MY DESIRES EXERCISE

Below are examples of desires that are an expression of values. When you express your true desires, you are living your own values. Remember to make your own list like the one below, or to make the chart on the previous page for this list.

Keep in mind that you are a unique expression of life, so the desires you live as an expression of your own values will be customized to you.

1. **Value – Productivity**

Desires I express in living my value of productivity:
Finishing my office work by 4 p.m., planning out our weekly meals, working in the garden, combining my errands.

2. **Value – Creativity**

Desires I express in living my value of creativity:
Working on the kids' scrapbook, designing the logo for my client, telling my daughter a bedtime story, shopping at the home improvement store.

3. **Value – Adventure**

Desires I express in living my value of adventure:
Not booking our hotel rooms ahead of time, looking at the map for our bike trip, learning to ride a motorcycle, reading the new mystery novel by my favorite author.

4. **Value – Beauty**

Desires I express in living my value of beauty:
Working in the rose garden, watching the sky change colors, picking out my outfit for the party, flipping through the fashion magazine at the grocery store.

5. **Value – Prosperity**

Desires I express in living my value of prosperity:
Having my extended family over for dinner, picking fruit off our tree in the backyard, shopping at the farmer's market, checking my bank statement.

6. **Value – Focus**
Desires I express in living my value of focus:
Working on my model in the garage, reading my favorite poetry book, meeting my friend for coffee, experimenting with the new bread recipe.

7. **Value – Love**
Desires I express in living my value of love:
Walking my dog, sitting in the backyard, watching my son perform his solo, watching the news clip about the community coming together.

8. **Value – Playfulness**
Desires I express in living my value of playfulness:
Having our neighbors over for margaritas, shopping in the city, playing with my granddaughter, eating popsicles.

9. **Value – Honesty**
Desires I express in living my value of honesty:
Reporting all my income, sharing my feelings with my sister about what she said, making the decision to find a new roommate, keeping track of my calories.

10. **Value – Purposeful**
Desires I express in living my value of being purposeful:
Communicating I will no longer be on the committee, cleaning out the garage, responding to the call for a new job, meeting with my editor for an update meeting.

You may have the same or similar values as are listed in the above example. However your desires will most likely be completely different. Write your list, your own values expressed as your own desires, for yourself. Think and feel it all through as you do it.

How you shape and mold your life energy is unique to you. What is a pull for you may be a push for someone else and vice versa.

EXPLORING DESIRES

The information you have been collecting and sorting through so far may seem trivial to the discovery of your authentic self. But over time you will see that you are piecing together the picture of your true self.

Your pushes and pulls reveal information personal to you. This is why your journal is so important. At first what you are discovering may appear to be all over the place without any consistency, or perhaps may just seem trivial. But over time, while working with your information about the patterns and themes you resonate strongly with, the authentic you will begin to emerge. With this awareness, you will know yourself better and you will feel yourself coming back to life.

Take a moment to go back and look at the pushes/pulls you recorded in Step 1. Then look at the values your pulls revealed to you as you recorded these in Step 2. Now, see here in Step 3 how you are learning about your desires, the desires you have expressed or want to express.

Some of the information you are seeing you may have already known about yourself. Other information you will be gaining from the five exercises, one exercise in each of these 5 Steps, may appear new to you. Basically, you are discovering or rediscovering who you are.

Parts of you may seem new to you as you do these exercises. However, you are already here, just waiting to be recognized by yourself. This information is important to know because it helps you have a greater understanding of who you are.

In general, when you are being pulled, when this pull is strong and basic, you are being driven by a real personal value and you are following a true desire. But when you are feeling that other sensation, that pushing against feeling, this is an indication that you are resisting the flow.

You will learn to more and more feel the difference between (a) being pulled toward something and (b) pushing against something.

If you say yes to following your shoulds, this is a push. And if you don't say yes but feel you should have said yes, you still feel a push. There is no true desire in having a should direct you. This becomes a lose/lose scenario.

You will see that shoulds do not direct your true desires. You will come to know that your life is designed to work. We will get to this in Step 5: CHOOSING YOUR BIGGER YES, but for now it is helpful to just become familiar with what it feels like to follow your desires and live your values.

WHEN INNER CONFLICT ARISES

We cannot live out a push and a pull simultaneously. We might feel as if we are being both pushed and pulled at the same time. But in any one moment we are living out either the pull or the push. Yet we may however blend together our sense of that push feeling and that pull feeling.

Of course, the feeling of being pushed and pulled at the same time can be quite troubling. In fact, we are likely to be experiencing pretty intense inner conflict when feeling both pushed and pulled. These two energies, the energies of the pushes and of the pulls, can feel as if they are crashing into one another. If you ever feel that your pushes and pulls are colliding with each other, you are picking up on the tug of war going on inside you. Just remember to:

**know that your authentic self
wants to go with the flow.
However a thought you are engaged in
may be holding you back.**

One moment you find yourself inspired and energized as you are tuning into your true desires. And then the next, your energy drops. You may feel embarrassed or doubtful and wonder why you ever considered such a crazy idea in the first place. What just happened?

What happened here is this: a thought that you could not be your authentic self intersected with a true desire you have. So you were blocked and your true desire had nowhere to go. When this sort of thing happens, you do feel like you are stuck – because you are indeed stuck. You have run into resistance. Your engine has temporarily stalled. In the moment this happens, you are not feeling your connection to life or to yourself, you are feeling separate and powerless.

If you believe you can't flow your energy in the direction it wants to go, that you can't do what you are truly being pulled to do, then your energy will find another place to flow. When your energy is stuck, blocked, it may look for a self-destructive outlet in the form of a bad habit or maybe a damaging behavior harmful to yourself or to others.

When you can't find a way through to be your authentic self, you may become depressed or find yourself acting out in unhealthy ways. The good news is that the flow of life is always there waiting for you to recognize and remember it. Even if you are feeling helpless, powerless, depressed, angry, or frustrated, all is not lost.

All is never lost.
Our own good,
what is ours
to have, to do and to be,
awaits
our receptivity.

Remember there is wisdom in your resistance, in your pushes. The only reason you are feeling resistance is because life is calling you forth and it appears you can't go. There is more life flow that wants to be expressed through you and as you. You wouldn't feel that stuck resistant energy, that push, if there weren't a true desire that was trying to be expressed by you.

The stuck sensation and the inner conflict you may sometimes feel with this, can lead you to your truest self. This is because the sense of being stuck points to the exact spot where you feel your happiness is being denied you. It is as if your mind is trying to convince you that you don't deserve to be happy, that you cannot be your authentic self.

In the next step, Step 4: UNDERSTANDING YOUR RESISTANCE, you will recognize the patterns that are attempting to block the flow of your good. With this awareness, you will be able to make different choices that will allow you to come out and once again participate fully in life, in your life.

23
Step Four: Understanding Your Resistance

So now after these first three steps, you're feeling good. You're in the flow, having a good time, enjoying the people around you. And then, boom, you run into resistance. Your energy drops, you feel separate, small, invisible, powerless.

What just happened? Where did your attention go? An event or a thought occurred that caused you to doubt or to judge yourself. Look closely at what just happened.

When you look, you may at first think you are judging the circumstances or the people around you. But looking to see what is going on is not judging. You may feel that just by looking at what is going on, you are judging the people around you.

However, if you look a little more closely, you will see the one you are judging or diminishing is yourself. You are thinking that you did or said something wrong. Your mind went to its calculating place of adding up your inadequacies. You think to yourself that in that moment something happened and things fell apart, that you did something wrong to make that moment happen the way it did. Or perhaps you are thinking that there is something wrong with you, that if you feel the way you do there is an inherent flaw in you.

Do not worry about this. Thoughts like these are not unusual. Just pay attention to what is going on within you. If you hit upon a diminishing thought – or maybe a better way to say this is when a diminishing thought hits you – you respond. And your response will vary based on your personality. If you have the personality that often blames others when you feel diminished, you may lash out at those others. And if you have the personality that often blames yourself when you feel diminished, you may tear yourself apart. It doesn't matter what your tendency may be, either way you are left feeling separate from the flow.

Even though the expression of your pain may be different depending on your personality, your pain stems from the same…

root cause:

having a misunderstanding
of
the truth of
who you are.

When we diminish ourselves or feel powerless, this is an indication we have run into resistance. The resistance we are experiencing is not necessarily a bad thing. This serves as a wake up call, alerting us that we are drifting further and further away from our true selves.

We resist our lives when we don't have an understanding of the way through our situations, and through our feelings about those situations.

When diminishing thoughts surface, these can stop us in our tracks. With understanding, we can redirect our energy and get back into the giving and receiving flow. Once we have an understanding of what causes our resistance, what the pushes we feel are telling us, then the mystery of why our lives feel the way they do is solved.

As we drift away from awareness of our authentic selves, we lose perspective and can't see what is true and what is not. We begin to gather evidence that supports what we think we see and this distorts our vision.

You may have experienced something like this. A situation may start off with a subtle or slight discomfort. Someone may have given you a look that you interpreted to mean he or she is not interested in what you are saying.

This can then escalate to "well I don't think he (or she) is very interesting either." And then you find more fault with that person, almost a retaliation. Before you know it, you are thinking that there is something wrong with everybody. If you follow the thread back to your original discomfort, you will see that it originated with you diminishing yourself as a result of something, in this case, a look someone gave you.

WHY DO WE DIMINISH OURSELVES?

We diminish ourselves when we are not familiar with our innate goodness and wholeness. We live in a society where the focus is very much outer directed. We are bombarded with information about and images of the "right" way to be. While we are growing up this sort of message comes from all directions – our parents, teachers, the media, friends, etc. This is part of the incessant self improvement model that lets us know that we are not quite there yet, not quite good enough, not quite something enough.

This is the vicious **cycle of not enough**. We are not thin enough, not rich enough, not clever enough, not secure enough, not smart enough, not ambitious enough, not giving enough, not popular enough, not beautiful enough, not creative enough, not nice enough, not healthy enough, not spiritual enough, *simply not enough.*

The not enough cycle is insatiable. There are billons of people on the planet. Why do we feel that if we are not superior to others in at least one category, usually more than one category, we are less than? We will always be less than something if we let this message run us. Winning the less than game is impossible.

This not-enough less-than thing
is a set up.
This is
why all of this can feel so defeating.
We lose that game
before we even
get out of bed in the morning.

However, we cannot lose at
the *real* game:
the game of already being enough.

We are already enough.
Each of us is.

YOU HAVE ALREADY WON

You have already won the game of life because you carry within you your authentic self. As you more and more focus within yourself and embrace who you truly are, who you are becomes more and more clear. The values you are and the seeds of desire that have been planted within you are there. You can express these. Even though you may have thought you had to be clever like your Uncle, ambitious like your friend, or easy going like your neighbor, you realize that you don't want to live another's life. You love the life you have been given to live, the life you are perfectly designed to live to its fullest expression.

You really don't want to live another person's life or the set of circumstances that make up that other person's life. Sure, there may be aspects of another's life that inspire you, but you wouldn't want to swap the whole package. When another person's life inspires you, it is important to notice why.

Think about this. What exactly about another person's life is an inspiration to you? Once you recognize the value that the other person is expressing, you can look inside yourself to see whether that value lives within you. Does that value inside you want to see the light of day?

Your expression of this value may be different from someone else's expression of this value, yet another person's expression of this value can be an inspiration to you. There may also be times when you look at someone else who can be an inspiration to you, but instead you feel diminished.

Before we further explore why you personally would diminish yourself here, it is important to repeat some of what we discussed earlier in this book.

There is a
knowing within you
that is
constantly guiding you
to what is
best for you.

However, if you are living in a scarcity consciousness, a less-than sense, it is difficult to see and feel this knowing within you. This is scarcity consciousness at work, having you believe that there is a finite supply and not enough for everyone: There is only so much to go around, so much love, so much money, so much success, so much acknowledgement. And if someone has more than you, you interpret this to mean there will be less available for you.

Limiting beliefs like these are everywhere. Of course, we can buy into these, we can believe these, if we wish to. We can also find ourselves caught in these when we do not wish to be. And, quite often we do not even see ourselves buying into these.

We sometimes even mistake these limiting beliefs for our own values. However, on some deep level we know, we always know, when these limiting beliefs do not match our own values. We feel this mismatch as dissatisfaction, agitation, exhaustion, depression, anger, or in other ways.

When limiting beliefs tell us that there is a scarcity – not enough love, or energy, or opportunity – we can find ourselves falling onto what I call the *scarcity track.*

If you are on the scarcity track, you will feel justified and right in your not-enough less-than thinking. However, from that perspective you will not be able to experience the abundance that is awaiting your recognition. You just won't have access to it unless you recognize this abundance is already here, within you.

Sometimes the concept of abundance is hard to accept. You may try to intellectually grasp this concept that life is abundant and is designed to work. And you may then find that it can be difficult to fully grasp this perspective, especially when you see scarcity. You'll gather evidence of all the limitations in your life and in yourself to prove you are right. You may also convince yourself you see evidence that someone else's behavior causes you to have less.

And you'll have plenty of evidence of how someone else's beliefs cause you to think less of yourself, to believe you are less than. Watch out for these beliefs as they are quite limiting.

KNOW THE DIFFERENCE BETWEEN LIMITING BELIEFS AND VALUES

It is important to see the big difference between values and limiting beliefs. Quite often we give ourselves, or receive from others around us, what may ***seem*** to be values. However, when we look closely these are not our values, these are instead beliefs that come to us for various reasons.

Of course many of our beliefs are wonderful and quite expansive beliefs, and they support us in being our authentic selves. Yet sometimes beliefs are not expansive and are instead limiting beliefs. We hear and digest these limiting beliefs and then inaccurately believe that these are the truth of who we are, the truth about us and what we value. Most likely we heard such diminishing thoughts from people around us when we were growing up, people in authority. We didn't think to question how these other people were defining us. And this way of accepting limiting beliefs about ourselves may have stayed with us into adulthood.

In this book and in these 5 Steps to your authentic self and life, we are working to see the difference between our own values and any limiting beliefs we may have. In this book we use the word "values" to define the truth of who we are. Values are what are most important to us, what we hold most important in our lives, and what we love most about ourselves – about our authentic selves. Our values are the essence of who we really are. Our values are inclusive and contain our wholeness. Our values do not diminish us in any way.

When we have an awareness of our values, we can more easily detect the presence of any limiting beliefs at work on us, in us or around us. And with this mindfulness we can stop the invasion of limiting beliefs.

We can stop limiting beliefs from identifying us in a way that lessens our value as human beings.

LIMITING BELIEFS ←
are the opposite of your
→ VALUES

GET READY TO SAY YES TO YOURSELF

So until you yourself have the experience of consciously making the decision to say yes to the flow of life, you will not fully know that you are already there, already part of this flow. Finding this out for yourself is going to take a little faith. You are going to have to try and work with the exercises I am suggesting in this book to have your own experience of being in the flow.

**Then faith in this flow
will be yours.**

Your abundance lives in the giving and receiving flow. There is no fear and scarcity in this flow. Any fear and scarcity you are experiencing is either a misunderstanding of your own, or a misunderstanding coming to you from outside yourself. These misunderstandings are causing you to believe you are separate from the flow.

So, if everything you want to experience in this lifetime lives in the flow, why wouldn't you live in that consciousness every moment of every day? In this Step 4 part of the journey, this step to your authentic life, you will discover why you are not allowing yourself permission to fully live in the flow.

You will uncover why you don't entirely believe you deserve to be fully in the flow. You will see why you may feel less than, even unworthy of, the chance to be the fullest expression of who you are, of the love that you are:

**love for yourself,
for your authentic self
and for who you truly are.**

The following pages will take you through the four part process of the *Step 4: UNDERSTANDING MY RESISTANCE EXERCISE.* This exercise begins with your pushes.

Step 4
UNDERSTANDING MY RESISTANCE EXERCISE
Part 1: Review Pushes

Go back to your journal, start a new page there, and write down your strongest pushes of the week. First, review these examples:

Pushes: *Things I was doing or thinking when I felt an inner conflict, or when I felt a sensation of pushing against myself or others:*

1. *When Michael, who I am working on a project with, didn't return my phone call;*
2. *Talking to my friend about her retirement plans;*
3. *Agreeing to be the treasurer of our club;*
4. *Noticing a colleague's hourly rate on his website;*
5. *Not having the money to pay off my credit card;*
6. *My boss scheduled a late afternoon meeting which means I may miss my bus;*
7. *Hanging up my new clothes.*

The items you put on your pushes of the week list are places where you felt some form of resistance. Again, as I have said earlier, this resistance can be something you feel to be coming from within you or from outside of you. Just be aware of the sensation of pushing against, resisting, both your own stuff and that coming at you from other people.

Step Four
Understanding My Resistance Exercise Chart

Step 4
Understanding My Resistance Exercise

My Push (my resistance)	The Should	The Rule	The Limiting Belief
______________	______________	______________	______________
______________	______________	______________	______________
______________	______________	______________	______________
______________	______________	______________	______________
______________	______________	______________	______________
______________	______________	______________	______________
______________	______________	______________	______________
______________	______________	______________	______________
______________	______________	______________	______________
______________	______________	______________	______________
______________	______________	______________	______________

If you feel yourself pushing against the flow and resisting, just know this: your authentic self is involved. We are now going to go on through the four part process of understanding resistance. This will help you understand why someone, why you, may run into resistance. The information that is used in this exercise is gathered from your list of pushes. Before beginning, find on the previous page the chart you will make to do this exercise.

Step 4
UNDERSTANDING MY RESISTANCE EXERCISE
Part 2: Notice the Word Should

Go back to the list of your pushes. Think about each push you have listed there. Listen to what your pushes are saying. Chances are that each of your pushes will either have the words "should" or "should not" in it, or will carry a should or should not meaning in it. These meanings may be something you tell yourself you should or shouldn't have done, said, felt, or wanted. Basically the message is that "there is something wrong with the way I am."

This is not always clear to us at first. So here, I will demonstrate how to recognize shoulds in your pushes. As I said earlier, your pushes and pulls are unique to you. What your own pushes and pulls are, and what these mean to you, will always be unique. So where I offer examples of these, as I do below, keep in mind that these are not necessarily your own pushes or your own interpretation of these pushes. These are just examples.

Remember, we are just using these other people's pushes to show how to gather valuable information from your own pushes. You will have the opportunity to work through your own pushes later.

Examples of the Shoulds in Our Pushes Listed for the UNDERSTANDING MY RESISTANCE EXERCISE

1. When Michael, who I am working on a project with, didn't return my phone call – *I shouldn't have to rely on other people.*

2. Talking to my friend about her retirement plans – *I should have planned my life better.*

3. Agreeing to be the treasurer of our club – *I know bookkeeping so I should do it.*

4. Noticing my colleague's hourly rate on his website – *I should charge more for my services.*

5. Not having the money to pay off my credit card this month – *I should pay off my credit card every month.*

6. My boss scheduled a late afternoon meeting which means I may miss my bus – *I shouldn't say anything.*

7. Hanging up my new clothes – *I shouldn't have bought new clothes.*

Now, on a page of your journal, again write down the top pushes you have experienced recently or are presently experiencing. Next to each of these pushes, write down a should or should not you connect with the push. Where you are not sure, just try to find a should or should not that might relate to the push on some level. If you need to think about this using other words, try these other words for should and should not: ought to, ought not to, better to, better not to.

We all have words for the shoulds we think are coming at us, and also for the shoulds we are giving ourselves. Just find words that say should to you, and then add a should or something like a should to each of the pushes you list for this step of this exercise.

In this part of the exercise, all you need to do is identify the should or the should not you are hearing, or the should/should not you are telling yourself. It is important that this should or should not be about you. It is not about what you think other people should or should not do. This is about you and the shoulds you feel are affecting you. It is important that your focus stay on you here.

Inside of every push is a diminishing thought. But why would we diminish ourselves, why would we berate ourselves with the statements: I should, or I should not? Or I am not enough because I do not, or I am not?

Why do we think our lives or ourselves should be different from what they truly are? This takes us to the next part of this four-part Step 4 exercise….

ABOUT RULES

The reason we are saying we should or shouldn't have done, said, felt, or wanted something is because we think we broke a "rule." Even though most of these rules aren't being spoken, not being spoken directly to us, we live as if they are. Quite often, we are given – either directly or indirectly – rules aimed at keeping us in line.

Yes, many rules exist to help us survive in the world, or at least to seem as if they are helping us survive. The problem with most of these rules is that they are based on fear and scarcity states of mind and beliefs. Yet these fear and scarcity states of mind and beliefs can keep us out of the flow of life, out of the flow of ourselves – out of our authentic selves.

Growing up, a "rule" I was taught by my mother was, "Always let the boys win at swimming." The way I interpreted this rule through the years was "don't be powerful, do not be yourself around men. Play small, dumb, incompetent so that men will feel important about themselves and continue to take care of you."

You can see how loaded rules like these can be. Most of the time, these rules are expressed to us in the form of some casual statement. Yet if you look within, deep inside this rule coming at you, you will see unspoken meaning. You will see either meaning you felt was coming at you, or meaning you made up.

Another rule I heard was, "Be nice to everyone because you never know who your boss will be." On the surface this may not sound very harmful. Being nice is a good thing, right? Yet the message I picked up from this rule was one that said: other people are my source so I had better not mess with my relationships with them. Basically, if I am not nice, then I will not get what I want and need. I am powerless to create my own reality, so I had better be nice to everyone just in case I may need any of them someday. In other words, "Don't burn your bridges."

Rules like these are telling you that "what you truly want and need is irrelevant," that "what is most important is that people like you and think highly or at least well of you." When I was growing up and even in the early years of my adulthood, the limiting belief I took from these rules I was given was this: I am powerless.

In my many years of coaching, I have experienced the wonderful goodness of people and their desire to do the right thing. The only problem with this is that …

people too often believe that to do the right thing is to not do the right thing for themselves.

If our lives reflect the rules and scarcity beliefs that we inherit or that are being imposed on us from outside ourselves, then our lives may not reflect our own values. When this is happening, we feel pain, conflict, confusion, and the feeling of being powerless.

Fortunately, our inner selves don't let this sort of error go by unnoticed. We feel this error. When something is not in alignment with our true self, we feel this – as a push.

The biggest problem with the rules is they lock us into a pattern of scarcity and our vision narrows. When we are caught in this pattern, we feel powerless to choose anything else. This feels like the end of the story for us: this is just the way life is so get used to it. Our energy drops as feelings of resignation, hopelessness and despair creep in.

A rule is spoken→

**You turn this spoken rule into
an unspoken rule →**

**You hear this unspoken rule in your mind
in the form of a should→**

**This should appears to be
coming from outside of you at you→**

You react to this should→

You feel resistance.

Step 4
UNDERSTANDING MY RESISTANCE EXERCISE
Part 3: Identify Unspoken Rules

Now go back to parts one and two of this exercise where you listed your pushes and the shoulds that go with them. Look at this list you made and think about any unspoken rules that are part of these.

In this part of the exercise, what we want to do is simply this: acknowledge that we have been living inside of a rule; and, identify what this rule is that is telling us why we should or shouldn't have done or felt something. Here are some examples of what people do with this part of this exercise:

1. *When Michael, who I am working on a project with, didn't return my phone call – I shouldn't have to rely on other people. – Don't ask for too much.*
2. *Talking to my friend about her retirement plans – I should have planned my life better – If you fail to plan, you plan to fail.*
3. *Agreeing to be the treasurer of our club – I know bookkeeping so I should do it - Everyone has to carry her or his own weight.*
4. *Noticing a colleague's hourly rate on his website – I should charge more for my services - If you value yourself, you charge a lot of money.*
5. *Not having the money to pay off my credit card this month – I should pay off my credit card every month – People who pay credit card interest are foolish.*
6. *My boss scheduled a late afternoon meeting which may cause me to miss my bus – I shouldn't say anything. – The boss is always right.*
7. *Hanging up my new clothes – I shouldn't have bought new clothes – Money doesn't grow on trees.*

There is a story about fleas in a jar. The fleas were trying to get out of the jar but they kept bumping into the lid.

At some point the lid was removed, but the fleas wouldn't fly above where the lid had been. They were trained to stop where the lid was so that even after the lid was removed, they wouldn't fly above it.

This is what happens to us. We become conditioned to live within these limiting beliefs and rules even though we are all grown up now and making our own decisions.

The rule is: don't fly above a certain height. This rule then turns into the belief: I can't fly above a certain height.

Step 4
UNDERSTANDING MY RESISTANCE EXERCISE
Part 4 – Discover Limiting Beliefs

In the first parts of this Step 4 Exercise, you have: (1) listed your pushes; (2) noticed the shoulds behind your pushes; and then (3) identified the rules behind those shoulds. Now, in part four of this Step 4 Exercise, it is time to see how you may have personalized those rules – taken those rules coming at you from outside yourself in to judge yourself by them. And you will understand more about your resistance.

Limiting beliefs are diminishing thoughts we hold about ourselves. These limiting beliefs are how we have personalized the unspoken rules we are living within, following. Limiting beliefs are communicating to us that we shouldn't be who we are, we shouldn't have done what we did, we shouldn't have felt what we felt, and/or we should have done or felt something other than what we did.

We may not even be aware that these beliefs are making decisions for us. These beliefs create an invisible barrier between us and our authentic selves. We often think we have to shape our behavior to fit inside of our limiting beliefs. We let limiting beliefs define us, put a lid on all we can be and do.

Many of our limiting beliefs came to us during childhood. Already as children, the culture, environment and or family structure we were part of gave us limiting beliefs about ourselves and life. Sometimes those beliefs were specific and sometimes they were more general.

Most of us continue to hear limiting beliefs coming at us during our adulthoods.

It is how we handle these messages of limitation coming at us that can make a difference in our lives.

It is important to know we resist limiting beliefs when these are not true limitations. We may feel this going on inside ourselves, but may not realize what is happening. Sometimes we do not notice this resistance. Or we may feel tense, or depressed, or confused, or we may feel pain of some sort. Much of this is the pain of resistance.

The pain of resistance is the pain of misunderstanding who we are – and of not allowing ourselves to be our authentic selves. We do not feel this pain of resistance because of a particular situation or issue although it may appear to us that we do. We may think that a particular situation is what is causing our discomfort, however, the pain runs deeper and is about much more.

The pain comes from knowing, knowing on some level, that we just sold out on ourselves.

Sometimes we sell out on ourselves on an ongoing basis. We sell out when we align our energy with our limiting beliefs instead of with our authentic selves. We also sell out on ourselves when we berate ourselves for the way we have chosen to live our lives.

For example, when we agree to be the treasurer of our club when we are already over committed, or when we criticize ourselves for wanting to throw our parents an anniversary party when we do not have the cash on hand to do so, or when we withhold our communication because we tell ourselves we do not have anything worth communicating – we may criticize ourselves for making these choices. Yet we may not realize what is going on inside us, what pushes we are feeling and why.

Basically we sell out on ourselves every time we follow a should or a should not which results in our feeling diminished, when we follow a should instead of our own values. It is in that moment of that push that we know we did not listen to or even hear our authentic selves, our true values. Instead we were identifying with our limiting beliefs, we were saying yes to our limiting beliefs by listening to the shoulds and following the rules. Instead of harmonizing with our true selves, with our authentic selves, we too often go into agreement with our limiting beliefs.

You know when this happens. It is as if you just hit a bad note. You feel this off note in the form of a push. When you feel a push, this is the wisdom within you alerting you. This push lets you know that in that moment you stepped out of harmony with your authentic self. This is why there is great wisdom in your pushes.

If you listen, you will realize that both your pushes and your pulls are always in the process of guiding you back to your true self.

Step Four
UNDERSTANDING MY RESISTANCE
Exercise Examples

Here we are going to explore examples of limiting beliefs. These are examples people have come up with when adding these to the lists made in the previous parts of this exercise:

1. When Michael, who I am working on a project with, didn't return my phone call – I shouldn't have to rely on other people – Don't ask for too much – I AM NEEDY.
2. Talking to my friend about her retirement plans – I should have planned my life better – If you fail to plan you plan to fail – I AM A FAILURE.
3. Agreeing to be the treasurer of our club – I know bookkeeping so I should do it – Everyone has to carry his or her own weight – I AM LAZY.
4. Noticing a colleague's hourly rate on his website – I should charge more for my services – If you value yourself, your prices will reflect that – I DO NOT VALUE MYSELF.
5. Not having the money to pay off my credit card bill this month – I should pay off my credit card every month – People who pay credit card interest are foolish – I AM FOOLISH.
6. My boss scheduled a late afternoon meeting which may cause me to miss the bus – I shouldn't say anything – The boss is always right – I AM UNIMPORTANT.
7. Hanging up my new clothes – I shouldn't have bought new clothes – Money doesn't grow on trees – I AM IRRESPONSIBLE.

Reading the above examples, we can identify how the unspoken rules became personalized. For example:

1. I AM NEEDY…
   is a personalization of the rule that says:
   If you ask for too much, you are needy.

2. I AM A FAILURE …
   is a personalization of the rule that says:
   If you fail to plan, you are a failure.

3. I AM LAZY …
   is a personalization of the rule that says:
   If you do not carry your own weight, you are lazy.

4. I AM OF NO VALUE …
   is a personalization of the rule that says:
   If other people charge more than you, you do not value yourself.

5. I AM FOOLISH…
   is a personalization of the rule that says:
   If you pay credit card interest, you are foolish.

6. I AM UNIMPORTANT …
   is a personalization of the rule that says:
   What the boss wants is more important than your needs, you are unimportant.

7. I AM IRRESPONSIBLE …
   is a personalization of the rule that says:
   Money doesn't grow on trees and if you believe it does, you are irresponsible.

NOTE ABOUT UNSPOKEN RULE BREAKING

When we break or think about breaking a rule or an unspoken rule, we may, and often do, come to the conclusion that something is wrong with us. We did something wrong. We are less than.

Of course much or most of this is going on inside us subconsciously. When we really look at what is going on, when we shine the flashlight of awareness on the situation, when we look at it objectively and with grown up eyes, then we see more. We see our authentic selves trying to speak.

If you look closely at the rules you follow or think you should follow, and at how you interpret those rules for yourself, you will notice many of those rules go against your values. When these rules go against your values, you feel conflict, often deep inner conflict.

At first, this experience of seeing our authentic selves may make little sense to us, we may not realize what we are seeing, not in full anyway. This is alright.

What we want to do first is get to know ourselves, get to recognize our pushes and pulls, and then our values, and then our desires, and then see more about what we resist and what it feels like when we resist. This is all part of the path of your authentic life and of making the decision to choose your bigger yes.

24
Step Five: Choosing Your Bigger Yes

STEP 5: CHOOSING YOUR BIGGER YES is all about the healthy choices we can make – the choices we can make to empower us and support us in living authentic and happy lives.

When we live our lives following the shoulds coming at us from the outside world or even from within our own minds, we are following spoken and unspoken rules that may or may not express our own true values. When we are not doing what our authentic selves want to do, desire to do, what we are doing is choosing a lesser yes, *answering to a lesser yes.*

YOUR LESSER YES

The lesser yes is a yes, but it is a compromised yes. It is the yes we are agreeing to because we don't believe we can live our bigger yes, or because we may not even be aware that we have a bigger yes. We default to our lesser yes when we are unaware of a better more healthy choice, or because we don't believe we deserve to have what we really want or to be who we truly are. We compromise and sell out when we feel it's the best we can do.

For example, if you are living inside of the belief "I am unlovable," you may settle for a less than satisfying relationship believing you are just lucky that someone, anyone, will have you. Your bigger yes in this situation may be to end the relationship or it may be to heal the limiting belief that says "I am unlovable."

Another interesting thing about the lesser yes is that we often choose it believing it will eventually take us where we want to go. You may hear yourself saying, "I don't really want to get involved with this group, but if I don't make the effort I may miss out on a good business opportunity." We move forward with the action even if it doesn't feel right, hoping it will pay off down the road.

Another thing that is interesting about the lesser yes is that we often don't follow through with the lesser yes. We tell ourselves we should get involved with the group, but in truth we don't really want to so we don't. In this case, we are not choosing the bigger yes, which may be finding groups that align with our values. But we are also not choosing the lesser yes here. In this sort of situation, we can really feel how stuck our energy is.

When we pick our lesser yes we are going into agreement with one or more of our limiting beliefs. These beliefs can be very sneaky and slippery in their attempts to diminish us. We may hear ourselves saying, "I can't even get my lesser yes right, what makes me believe I deserve my bigger yes."

You probably wouldn't be using exactly those words. What you say to yourself may sound something more like, "If I can't even complete an article, what makes me think I can write a book."

And, in this example, when you choose to *deny your lesser yes,* you are not denying the article. You are denying the belief that is blocking you from writing the article. If you feel stuck writing an article or a book you want to write, there is likely a push and a limiting belief present.

You'll want to go in and release the misunderstanding you are holding about yourself. If you are stuck writing an article in particular, this in no way means you are incapable of writing a book. This is just another version of a limiting belief trying to convince you that you are limited.

Think a moment about this lesser yes. Too often, we are saying yes to thoughts, words and actions that do not align with our own values and desires. We are saying yes to limiting beliefs, often settling for the false sense of security that comes from doing what the lesser yes tells us to do. Yes, sometimes a sense of rightness comes with acting on the lesser yes, however this sense is not lasting as it is not really expressing our true selves.

Now think about your bigger yes. This is in no way your lesser yes. There are very clear differences between lesser and bigger yeses once we start really paying attention. Choosing your lesser yes can feel all right in the short term.

Yet this lesser yes action is a short term decision that frequently reveals itself as just a booby prize. Sure, we keep hoping and wishing that acting on our limiting beliefs will deliver what we want. Yet what we truly want is not delivered to us when we choose the lesser yes, because what we truly want does not come to us by diminishing ourselves.

The track of your limiting beliefs differs completely from the track of your authentic self.

Limiting beliefs →
choosing your lesser yes →
short term fix
that does
not satisfy.

Choosing your own values →
choosing your bigger yes →
long term expression
of your true self
that brings
satisfaction.

In working with the *5 Steps to An Authentically Happy Life* you can come to know the difference between choosing your lesser yes and choosing your bigger yes. What it means to answer to your bigger yes will become more and more clear to you.

Just know that your own bigger yeses will be more and more obvious to you. Do not be concerned if you take a while to truly feel the difference between your lesser and your bigger yeses.

Just know that
answering to your bigger yes
is saying yes to yourself,
to your authentic self.

Your bigger yes says yes to desires that reflect your truest values. This is what we are working on here in Step 5. You know you are on the path of your authentic self when you recognize your own values and express these in your true desires, when you choose your bigger yes.

KNOW WHAT CHOOSING A LESSER YES FEELS LIKE

As I explained earlier, your pushes are valuable teachers. There is real wisdom in your pushes. Become more and more aware of what your pushes feel like. When you are pushing against should-like messages coming at you from within or from outside yourself, you feel yourself resisting.

Notice yourself resisting when you are. Notice that you feel your resistance when you nevertheless do exactly that which you are on some level pushing against. So you do feel it when you are choosing your lesser yes.

Watch for times when you feel you are pushing against, resisting, something. You will get to know this feeling better and better. While you are busy resisting the flow, listening to limiting beliefs, your true desires are trying to get your attention. Be aware of what you are feeling when this is going on.

Remember, you won't feel resistance when you are expressing a true desire, choosing your bigger yes. However, if you are feeling resistance, then the communication is that your true, authentic desire wants to be expressed instead of the actions you are taking or the thoughts you are engaging in. Even while choosing your lesser yes,

your
authentic desire
is calling you forth.

On some deep level, we do know what we truly think and feel, and we do know what we truly desire to do and be. Yet limiting beliefs stop us, or we tend to let these stop us, from being our true selves, from thinking our true thoughts, from answering the call of our true desires. We just can't say yes to life when we are saying no to ourselves.

Get to know your lesser yes.

Get to a place where you can notice when you are choosing your lesser yes so you can slow down your thought process. This will give you time to pause, to know what you are feeling, and to make a different decision. The lesser yes reflects things we think or do based on the shoulds we hear. Many shoulds such as these are quite common:

I should play small;
I should do what they want;
I should want more;
I should be happy with the way things are;
I should be satisfied with all this;
I shouldn't feel this way;
I shouldn't say anything.

If you are taking action to follow your shoulds at the expense of your true desires, you will pay a price. And you will sure know you are paying the price by the way your life feels.

Initially you may not realize this is what is happening, you may not realize you are paying the price. After all, on the surface, it may appear that you are being good, nice, accommodating. And it may seem that you have actually even accomplished some of your goals – if your goals include feeling like this while you accomplish them.

Yet if your actions are not a reflection of your truest values, if what you do is not a reflection of who you truly are, of what is most important to you, then the satisfaction you feel will be a fleeting satisfaction. This sort of satisfaction is not authentic, and it comes and goes. With false satisfaction, you don't experience the true fulfillment and inner peace that is truly yours to have.

GET READY TO CHOOSE YOUR BIGGER YES BY LOOSENING THE GRIP OF YOUR LIMITING BELIEFS

At this point you may be wondering why you would ever choose your lesser yes when your bigger yes is waiting for you. The answer is quite simple: you choose your lesser yes because your limiting beliefs want you to.

Your limiting beliefs threaten you in order to encourage you to believe them.

Your limiting beliefs threaten you with things such as loss, telling you that you will lose something you value (such as love, or your job, or money, or your connection with certain people). There is always an element of seeming scarcity attached to your limiting beliefs.

Reaching a place where you fully get what I am saying here takes time. Do not worry about how much of this you completely understand at this moment. Give yourself time to learn what all this is about. Just keep working with the 5 Steps in this book, and in time, it will all come together for you. When you are working with your personal data, the process will become much clearer to you.

And do be very gentle with yourself when looking at, and working with, your limiting beliefs. Don't be too hard on yourself when you see what limiting beliefs you have fallen for. Just notice these.

Try to have compassion for yourself when you see...

...you have taken the bait and swallowed a bunch of limiting beliefs.

Of course, the temptation will be to judge yourself for doing or for not doing what limiting beliefs have been telling you to do or not to do. However, being hard on yourself will just keep you stuck. You do not want to stay stuck. You want to be released from the stuck condition so that you can live in the flow of life.

We all do have the desire to live in the flow of life. We are all feeling the pull to live in this flow. Of course, this doesn't mean we won't ever be bouncing back and forth between our lesser and our bigger yeses.

Yet, each time we have the awareness that we are choosing our lesser yes, or are about to choose our lesser yes, there is the opportunity to make a different decision, to choose our bigger yes. And, very often we don't even know we have chosen our lesser yes until our awareness opens to a greater possibility. We can still move on to new bigger yeses.

It is important to remember that you cannot get this process wrong. All roads lead you back to your authentic self. This is a journey, the journey of your life. So be gentle with yourself.

You will most certainly get back to experiencing the flow by practicing understanding, compassion and forgiveness along the way. These attitudes toward yourself as well as toward others will help you.

THE PRACTICE OF UNDERSTANDING...

Let's talk about understanding now. Understanding involves having information and awareness about what is really taking place. Quite often, when we become aware that we are thinking and acting based on a limiting belief, we feel powerless to do anything about it. We look at the limiting belief that is at work, and we may then become discouraged by seeing it. We may see that the limiting belief just sits there as if it is true. Even if we know it is not true, we can find it difficult to see any possibilities beyond it. This is because this limiting belief is so strong and has been with us for so long.

Just know that you can look objectively and calmly at your limiting beliefs. As you do, you can use more neutral phrases about these beliefs such as, "this is so interesting." This will help you see deeper into the belief. For example, "It is so interesting that I believe it is never my turn. Why do I believe this? When do I first remember coming to this conclusion?"

If you are able to separate yourself from the belief, you will gain more clarity. For example, it may be that your older sister excelled at everything, your parents were constantly praising her and you felt it was never your turn. You were always waiting on her. Everything was always about her. With that insight, you can see how you continued that thought process throughout your life. You can see how you got into this way of thinking.

It was never your turn in school. It wasn't your turn when your friends were getting married and settling down. It wasn't your turn when you were passed over for work promotions. And the list may go on and on. So you may hold on to this limiting belief that it is never your turn throughout your adult life.

Once you see the lens you have been looking through, you can better understand how you got yourself into this way of thinking. You can then start to have compassion for yourself.

THE PRACTICE OF COMPASSION…

"Oh no wonder I feel it is never my turn. I have been living inside of the belief that I have to wait for everything and for other people to get what they want first. But I don't seem to ever get what I want. I can see how this feeling started with my sister, back when we were growing up. But I've been the one keeping this going all these years."

Think about this statement, or better yet the feeling behind it. You may see something like this in your own mind and experience. And note that you can see where this came from and that you have been keeping this feeling going all these years.

With this realization, with this process of looking at what you are feeling and where this comes from, you can start to feel compassion for yourself. You might say, "It was difficult always being in my sister's shadow. I can see why I came to this conclusion that it is never my turn. I can see why I have been telling myself this all these years."

Once you get to this place where you can look at a limiting belief you may have carried for a long time, you can feel compassion for yourself. Then this limiting belief will begin to loosen its grip.

Move slowly here. Sometimes when we first identify a limiting belief that has been with us for a long time, our initial reaction is to blame someone or something else. "He, she, or they did this to me." "This is my parent's fault, my sister's fault, my teacher's fault, etc."

Just keep in mind that people say all kinds of things to us throughout our lives. And we sure cannot control what other people think, say, or do. Their thoughts are their thoughts. Their words are their words. Their behavior is their behavior. What we do have control over is what we do with the information that comes at us, over what we ourselves think, say and do.

Now, in the case of being told we are less than, not worthy, inadequate, it is unfortunate that we may have taken the bait. Taken the bait? Yes, we take the bait when we believe their opinions. Then we build some portion if not all of our own identify around what others say, and around what we think others are saying. We do this when we don't have a strong sense of our own authentic selves and values.

What someone is saying to you really doesn't matter in your definition of yourself. What does matter is what you do with the information you receive. Are you listening to the words around you, or to the true knowing in your own heart and soul?

Be aware so that you can know what is and is not true for you. Be aware so you can know whether what others are saying, and whether what you are saying, are things that you are allowing to diminish yourself. These are false beliefs and have nothing to do with the authentic you.

When you start working on this fifth step to your authentic self, to *Choosing Your Bigger Yes*, you may find yourself having difficulty letting go of a limiting belief. If so, do not judge yourself. You see, if you judge yourself for having a limiting belief, you will continue to stay stuck. If you hear yourself saying, "I can't believe I've wasted my life waiting for other people to grant me my turn," just slow down and try feeling more compassion for yourself.

Once you are able to see through the eyes of compassion for yourself, to know you are working on this process, then your energy will begin to shift. Tell yourself, "Oh, no wonder I thought that." And once you are able to say this, then be sure to acknowledge how difficult or challenging this limiting belief has been for you. Let yourself say, "It is important I see how rough it has been for me to live inside that belief." Have understanding and compassion for yourself as you look at why you believed what you did.

I want to say this again and again: Do make an effort to find and have compassion for yourself, compassion for yourself when you find yourself hearing, feeling, thinking less-than thoughts about yourself. Give it time, and work with the 5 Steps in this book. Compassion for yourself and for others will lead you to an authentically fulfilled life.

You will see you can feel good about yourself, you can experience and love your authentic self.

THE PRACTICE OF FORGIVENESS...

Forgiveness is not something that is given prematurely. We often hear we should forgive and move on, but this sort of thinking just keeps us stuck in the should cycle.

Actually, forgiveness is not something we have to consciously do. If we are trying to forgive and we can't, we haven't yet had a deep enough understanding of our situation.

Instead of trying to jump ahead to forgiveness, to force forgiveness, it is much more effective to keep deepening your understanding of yourself and your situation. Keep looking at all of it from various angles. Stand back from the situation to see if this gives you greater clarity. Look at everything from many different angles.

If a limiting belief you have originated with your parents, ask yourself if they were afraid. Ask yourself what their consciousness was. Did your parents express and live mostly by their true selves or by their false, compromised, selves? Too often we listen to fearful people tell us who we are.

As a parent myself, I know how slippery this can be. Our intention is to protect our children. We want to shield them from harm and hurt. And as we attempt to do this, we often do come from a fearful place. Our original intention comes from love, yet very often our fears kick in. Then what we end up projecting to our children are our fears.

Once you have a greater understanding of your own and other people's situations, what naturally follows is compassion. Again, you don't have to try to be compassionate. Compassion will be the natural outcome of understanding. The same is true for forgiveness.

As you understand more, you will feel more compassion for yourself. With the softening effects of compassion for yourself, you will naturally begin to release yourself, to ***forgive yourself*** for living by those limiting beliefs. You will even forgive the beliefs themselves.

Once the feeling of compassion for yourself begins to flow through you, the grip of your limiting beliefs begins to release. As your compassion for yourself flows more and more, those limiting beliefs will have less and less a hold on you.

This is because your perception will be shifting. You will be able to understand why you came to the limiting conclusions that you did. Then you will be able to have more compassion for yourself. And then you will be able to forgive yourself and others for those limiting beliefs.

Know that you are the only person who has the power to forgive, to let go of, the limiting beliefs you have been living inside. Another person can't do this for you. Someone can say whatever he or she wants to you, but until you can see a possibility beyond the limiting beliefs, there will be no forgiveness.

Your decision to either keep living inside a limiting belief, or to live authentically in the flow of life, is a very personal choice you make. This is a choice between you and you.

Once you have a real understanding of, and a true compassion for, why you developed limiting thought patterns in the first place, you will realize you have the power to make different choices. With understanding, compassion, and forgiveness you are able to see the truth about yourself and your life more clearly. The fog lifts and you can actually see that you really like who you are, who you truly are, your authentic self.

You will love who you truly are, your true self, far more than you can love your compromised self. When you come face to face with yourself, you can recognize your goodness and can feel authentically happy. Now that you have a greater understanding of where your mind tends to go, it is time to choose your thoughts. You do have dominion over your thoughts. And you do have the power to decide what thoughts are going to occupy your mind.

Without the awareness of your limiting beliefs, there is little you can do to see beyond them. Without realizing what limiting beliefs you live by, you may think that all of your life is just the way life is. Yet once you are able to loosen the grip of limiting beliefs, to get out of that place, you can tune into your true desires. You can choose the bigger yes!

THIS IS AN ONGOING PROCESS

This step, Step 5: CHOOSING YOUR BIGGER YES, is about you making a decision to be yourself, your authentic self, and to allow yourself to live your authentic life.

To prepare for this step, you will want to move through the understanding, compassion and forgiveness process discussed on the previous pages. Your understanding, compassion and forgiveness for both others and yourself will help you as you choose the bigger yeses over the lesser yeses in your life.

To summarize here, let me say again that the importance of your having understanding, compassion and forgiveness as you move through Step 5 and choose your bigger yes is central. As you work through Step 5's ongoing process of choosing the bigger yeses in your life, you are asked to:

Have an *understanding* of why a particular limiting belief has been and is gripping you, and then…

With this deeper understanding of the origin of this limiting belief, you will experience *compassion* for yourself, and then…

With the softening that arises out of this compassion, you can experience forgiveness and *forgive* yourself, and in so doing…

You will then give up the grasp the limiting belief has on you, and…

Choose Your Bigger Yes.

This work is ongoing, continuous.

You may have been living inside your limiting beliefs for years. Those beliefs are not going to magically disappear once you get your first glimpse of them, once you first begin to work with these steps. The *5 Steps to An Authentically Happy Life* I present in this book can definitely form a lifelong and satisfying practice. You can always be more of yourself, and you can always find more of yourself by way of this 5 Step process.

CHOOSING YOUR BIGGER YES

Now that you have begun to release the grip that your limiting beliefs have had on you, it is time to consciously choose the thoughts that align with your authentic self. It is time to have an awareness of how your limiting beliefs have been making choices for you. With an expanded awareness, you are in a position to:

choose what you value
and what you do
based on the
desires of
your authentic self.

As I have explained, this choosing is not a one time occurrence. This is something you do moment by moment. Initially this may feel a bit mechanical because you are slowing down your thought process. But eventually, as you are more and more in the habit of living from your authentic self, your thoughts, words and actions will naturally align with your authentic self.

The Step 5 CHOOSING MY BIGGER YES EXERCISE will work with you along these lines. To begin this exercise, let's go through some of the examples we have been working with in this book. This will help you to have an idea of this choosing your bigger yes process.

So let's look again at the limiting beliefs we ended up with after working with pushes in Step 4:

1. I am needy;
2. I am a failure;
3. I am lazy;
4. I do not value myself;
5. I am foolish;
6. I am unimportant;
7. I am irresponsible.

These are just some of the many common limiting beliefs people may have about themselves. And it is within these limiting beliefs that we find quite common pushes. Again know that every time we notice – experience, feel, sense – a push, we can unravel it. We can look more and more deeply into this until we arrive at the limiting belief, the pocket of scarcity, that is located within it.

Once we are able to identify the limiting belief behind the push we are dealing with, we can see what sort of beliefs we are or have been living from. For example, if the lens we have been looking through is "I have nothing of value to contribute," then this is all we will be able to perceive. When we hold such a limiting belief, we gather evidence to prove we have nothing of value to contribute. We don't want to see that the evidence supporting this limiting belief is incorrect, so believing this limiting belief becomes a habit.

**We use this evidence
to support this limiting belief,
and therefore
keep living by this limiting belief.**

We do not actually want to live by this limiting belief. But in the moment, if we are not aware of our authentic selves, our own desires and values, it appears to us that we don't have a choice. All there seems to be for us is the limiting belief.

When we live on this sort of track, this limiting track, we end up frustrated and disappointed with the world because the world doesn't appreciate our contribution. We tell ourselves and the world that we are not appreciated.

By agreeing with the limiting belief, we are likely creating a situation for ourselves which is the exact opposite of what we truly desire.

You can see how this can become a catch-22. In my many years of coaching I have witnessed first hand how a person's limiting beliefs are often diametrically opposed to the truth of who she or he is.

> A person who has the belief "I am needy" is often quite secure.
>
> A person who has the belief "I am a failure" is often not disappointed with her or himself.
>
> A person who has the belief "I am lazy" is often quite ambitious.
>
> A person who has the belief "I don't value myself" often has a deep respect and appreciation for who she or he is.
>
> A person who has the belief "I am foolish" is often particularly wise.
>
> A person who has the belief "I am unimportant" often knows of her or his value.
>
> A person who has the belief "I am irresponsible" is often quite responsible.

These limiting beliefs may not make much sense to you when you see them at work in other people. But if you tune into *your* life and admit what you know to be true about *yourself,* you will understand what I am saying: Your own limiting beliefs are trying to convince you that their diminishment of you is true, but your authentic self knows better. That is why you feel an inner conflict between your authentic self and your compromised self.

As young children we were often criticized for the way we were. This may have been because our values didn't fit in with the rest of our family's values, or because our caregivers were afraid we wouldn't be safe being the way we were. So we tried to withhold our true selves, to be the kind of people others expected us to be.

If we had had a good sense of our own value, our caregivers might have felt we were becoming too big for our britches and they might have pointed out why we shouldn't be so confident. Or, if our intelligence threatened other family members, they might have tried to convince us we weren't so smart in order to make themselves feel more comfortable.

The reason these beliefs are so painful for us is that these beliefs do not represent the truth of who we are.

When we feel the pain of the mismatch between our true selves and our limiting beliefs, we are feeling the effects of having latched on. Yes, we have latched onto our limiting beliefs as if they are true. And, ever since we first latched on, we have been gathering evidence to support these limiting beliefs.

There is a way to break free of this incessant pattern, and this way is through awareness. By working through the steps in this book, you will develop the discernment needed to be able to choose the bigger yes in your life. You will be able to make the choices that reflect your authentic self.

When we find ourselves stuck and feeling outside the flow of life, it is time to make a new decision.

Too often, the thought patterns of our limiting beliefs have been practiced longer than the thought patterns of our own values, the values that are in alignment with our authentic selves. When this is the case, we will typically default to our limiting beliefs each time a choice has to be made – we will typically choose our lesser yeses.

Even though this decision to go with, to default to, our limiting beliefs may diminish us, there is a part of us that feels compelled to follow the "shoulds" and the "rules." This is therefore the decision we are making, the decision to stay stuck. However, we do not have to stay stuck.

The process of choosing the bigger yes is at first a bit like swinging on a trapeze. We swing back and forth, preparing to leap across. If the only thought we have around a particular situation is our limiting belief about that situation, we won't let go of the bar. If we did let go, we would be afraid of falling and getting hurt.

That limiting belief had originally been put in place to insure our survival. Yet when we know we have another bigger and better bar to reach for, when we know we will be safe when we reach for it, we will gladly release that lower bar. We will gladly release the lesser, the limiting belief, and reach for the greater bar, for our authentic desires and our own values.

You can't hold onto the bar of your limiting belief and simultaneously hold the bar of your bigger yes. If you try that, you will stay stuck in midair. You have to make a choice. What are you going to be loyal to: your limiting belief or your authentic self? Your limiting belief will eventually disappoint and frustrate you, while the other, your bigger yes, will bring you deep joy and satisfaction.

At first you may be hesitant to give up your limiting beliefs. You may feel that if you stop berating yourself, if you stop telling yourself you are not being or doing what you are expected to be and do, your life will really spiral out of control.

And yet it doesn't work that way.

What is keeping you stuck, keeping you in a place where you experience less than what you truly desire, where you live as your compromised self, is the power you have given your limiting beliefs. You have granted your limiting beliefs an inordinate amount of authority over yourself, an enormous power to tell you who you are.

Yet these beliefs do not allow much room for your authentic self to express and to be. Just look at the diminishing statements in your limiting beliefs and ask yourself: is this the truth of who I am? The answer is no.

At the moment, right now, this may not be crystal clear to you. Do not worry about this. You have probably been living inside of this limiting belief for quite awhile. And you may even have a tremendous amount of evidence that proves that this limiting belief is correct. But if this limiting belief is diminishing you in any way, it is not the truth of who you are.

You can stop gathering evidence for your limiting beliefs and begin to gather evidence for the real you. The more you live from your own values and desires, the more you see and feel the quality of your life improving, the more you see that your limiting beliefs are hogwash. They are lies that keep you chasing your tail.

So let's get into doing the Step 5 Exercise. This Step 5 Exercise uses everything you have learned in the first four steps. You will want to open your journal and write down your thoughts as you work through this step.

Step 5 Exercise, Part 1: Find Information in Pushes and Limiting Beliefs

Now it is time for you to make some decisions. However, before you can do this, you have to have a clear picture of your inner tug of war. What is the desire that wants to be birthed, expressed? What is the limiting belief that is trying to prevent this from happening?

Go back to your journal pages where you worked on Step 4. There you will find that you wrote down some of your pushes and then some of the shoulds, rules, and limiting beliefs you discovered inside of your pushes. Read these Step 4 notes over again and keep them out for use now, in Step 5.

As you read through your Step 4 Exercise list, think again now about your pushes and the limiting beliefs behind these. Your thinking will move you through it all again, somewhat like this example of other people's Step 4 work on the following page....

Examples of
Pushes to Limiting Beliefs Discovery
For the
CHOOSING MY BIGGER YES EXERCISE

1. When Michael, who I am working on a project with, didn't return my call – I shouldn't have to rely on other people – Don't ask for too much – I AM NEEDY.
2. Talking to my friend about her retirement plans – I should have planned my life better – If you fail to plan you plan to fail – I AM A FAILURE.
3. Agreeing to be the treasurer of our club – I know bookkeeping so I should do it – Everyone has to carry her or his own weight – I AM LAZY.
4. Noticing a colleague's hourly rate on his website – I should charge more for my services – If you value yourself, your prices will reflect that – I DO NOT VALUE MYSELF.
5. Not having the money to pay off my credit card bill this month – I should pay off my credit card every month – People who pay credit card interest are foolish – I AM FOOLISH.
6. My boss scheduled a late afternoon meeting which may cause me to miss my bus – I shouldn't say anything – The boss is always right – I AM UNIMPORTANT.
7. Hanging up my new clothes – I shouldn't have bought new clothes – Money doesn't grow on trees – I AM IRRESPONSIBLE.

The above list, or better yet, your own list like the one above (which you wrote in Step 4), results in your seeing some of your limiting beliefs such as: I AM A FAILURE, I AM LAZY, I AM UNIMPORTANT, and so on.

It is now time to look more deeply into this information you have gathered about yourself to see what is really going on. Keep in mind that your pushes reflect a moment in time.

While some of your pushes may be there over a longer period

of time, many of your pushes may change in the future – or may not be the same as other parts of your life change. For example, just because agreeing to be the treasurer of the club is a push for you this year doesn't mean it will not be a pull for you in a few years.

Remember it is the limiting belief that is causing the pain not the situation. Notice what it feels like if you deny the limiting belief and instead tell the truth about why you are resisting the should. Remember there is wisdom in your resistance. Your authentic self is alerting you that something is off. The rules are trying to convince you that you should be different from what you are or that you are doing something wrong.

Here are some statements taking the above examples to the next level, to releasing the false and claiming the truth. Of course, your statements will be very customized to you....

1. It is not true that I am needy. I resist doing this project myself because I am at my most creative when I am collaborating.
2. It is not true that I am a failure. I resist the thought that I should have planned my life better because I love the way my life has unfolded. I am spontaneous, flexible and love adventure.
3. It is not true that I am lazy. I resist agreeing to be the bookkeeper right now because I want to spend more time with my family.
4. It is not true that I do not value myself. I resist the idea of raising my prices because I am happy with my current price structure and want to make my work accessible to lots of people.
5. It is not true that I am foolish. I resist paying my credit card bill in full this month because I am planning an anniversary party for my parents.
6. It is not true that I am unimportant. I resist keeping quiet about having to work late because I want to get home in time to make dinner for my wife.
7. It is not true that I make poor choices. I resist the idea I shouldn't have bought new clothes because I wanted a new outfit for the party and I can afford it.

For now, you will be writing down your own pushes and the limiting beliefs behind your own pushes on the chart you will make for Step 5.

Go ahead and copy into your journal the blank Step 5 chart you find on the following page. Then on this Step 5 chart in your journal enter your Step 4 pushes in the first column on the left of this chart, and your Step 4 limiting beliefs in the second column from the left side of this chart.

Note: If you write in (there on your chart) your limiting beliefs as "I am" statements, you will be able to see how you have been falsely identifying yourself.

Step Five
Choosing My Bigger Yes
Exercise Chart

Step 5

Choosing My Bigger Yes Exercise

My Push	The Limiting Belief (False I Am)	My Desire	My Value (True I Am)	My Bigger Yes

Step 5, Part 2: Identify the Desire That Wants to be Birthed

You have written your pushes and limiting beliefs into the first two columns of your Step 5 chart. Now you are ready to work on the third column in your Step 5 chart. This is the desire column.

Remember, you would not be experiencing a push were there not also a desire present in the situation. We are always experiencing our desires, always on the desire track, whether or not we are realizing this. We are always living in the flow of life, however thoughts and feelings can surface that prevent us from experiencing being in the flow.

Sometimes something, some limiting or blocking thought, intersects our connecting with the flow. When this happens, we constrict our energy and feel we are not in the flow – we feel we are separated from the flow. The pain we feel is our longing to be back in the flow.

Take a moment and think about your pushes. Start with the first push on your list and then move to the next one. Before this push entered the picture, what was the desire track you were on? What were you truly desiring to express, do and be? You would not have been experiencing a push were there no values yearning to be expressed by desires. You are now at the fork in the road where it is time to make a decision.

But before you do this, it is important to identify the desire within you that wants to be birthed, expressed. In Step 3 you discovered some of your desires in your pulls. You can also uncover desires in your pushes. Whenever you find yourself resisting and pushing against, you can be sure there is a desire in there wanting to be set free.

Now, go back to your Step 5 chart. For each limiting belief you wrote down there, identify the desire that is being blocked by this limiting belief.

What is the desire you can't live out, can't express, because of the resistance you are experiencing? Write the desires that come to your mind down onto your Step 5 chart, in the Desires Column there.

Do not worry if the items you list on your Step 5 chart do not match up perfectly, you are brainstorming here, finding things out about yourself, about your authentic self.

Step 5, Part 3: Identify the Value That Longs to Be Expressed

Keep in mind that some of the desires you have are desires for what may seem to be little things in your life. These are things such as being home on time for dinner, talking about your project, planning a party, and so on. Just know that behind each of your desires are values, your own values. Also know that many seemingly small desires you have are about you expressing yourself, being yourself, and sharing the gift that you are.

So now let yourself look at whatever values behind your desires come to mind. Just notice what comes to your mind here. No need to explain it all to yourself at the moment. Over time, when you later repeat this step 5, you will uncover more about yourself and the values you have, the values that long to be expressed through your desires.

Now go to your Step 5 chart and find the values column there. Write the values you would be living were you following the desires you listed. Note: when you write in your values as "I am" statements, you will be expressing and feeling the energy of your true self.

This is because your true self, your I am, is who you are, and is a compilation of your values. Remember, on this Step 5 chart, write in your own examples. Be sure to add as many examples as you find in your own life whether you have two examples, or three or five or ten or more.

You decide. Also note that you can return to this exercise as often as you want, and you may want to add to your list or make new Step 5 charts each time.

On the following pages, there are examples of entries other persons have made on their Step 5 charts. You can read through these to see how pushes, limiting beliefs, desires, and then values are listed.

Again, your own examples will likely be different. Anything you feel you want to enter on your own chart is alright. Do not be concerned about getting any of this right or wrong. This is more like a brainstorming session you are having with yourself in order to get to know more about yourself.

Step 5, Part 4: Identify the Bigger Yes That is Asking to Be Answered Here

On the following pages where you find the Choosing My Bigger Yes Exercise Examples, you will see samples of other persons' entries into their Step 5 charts. You will see what their bigger yeses were.

You will see where each of these people has indeed chosen a bigger yes based on her or his desires and values.

Now, go to your own Step 5 chart. In each example of your own that you have written there, ask yourself what is the truth of who I am? Do you resonate more strongly with your false I am or your true I am?

Chances are it will be your true I am. However, if you have been living a long time predominantly as your false I am, it may take just a little while to get used to claiming your true self. I say just a little while because, deep down, your body, mind and soul already resonate with your true self.

Choosing Your Bigger Yes is aligning your thoughts, words and actions with your authentic self instead of with your compromised self. Your Bigger Yes may be the decision to take a certain action, to shift the inner dialogue you are having with yourself. Or it may just be a subtle feeling of relief as the thought washes over you that you are perfectly designed to fulfill your desires.

When you are listening to yourself, when you are uncovering the desires and values that are truly YOURS, you are also getting in touch with places where you may have been choosing your lesser yes, the yes that was attempting to satisfy your limiting beliefs.

Now that you can see this, you can see where there is another, bigger yes you can choose in each case. This is the choice only you can make for yourself. This is the choice only you know enough about yourself to make.

WHAT IS YOUR BIGGER YES?

It is now time for you to make a decision. Read through your Step 5 chart. In each situation you list as a push, what is the bigger yes for you?

What you will notice when you choose your bigger yes is that it really doesn't matter what caused the initial push. That initial push is not really about the particular circumstances or situation. Typically we want to blame other people for a push we are feeling.

So our first inclination is to feel we have to straighten those people out. It appears that they are the problem and need to be fixed. However with further exploration we realize the push we are feeling is not really about them or the situation. They and the situation were the catalysts that helped us realize that there are some unhealed wounds within us, some misunderstandings we are carrying about who we really are.

These unhealed wounds and misunderstandings about who we really are can be quite painful for us. This pain we feel is actually the belief that we are less than who we truly are. When we go into agreement with the lesser yes, the limiting belief, we are selling out on ourselves. This is what causes our pain.

When you feel this sort of pain, remember that you can ***Choose Your Bigger Yes*** for yourself. You can express this Bigger Yes through your thoughts, words and actions. This will bring you back to your authentic self, to your wholeness. And this is always your deepest desire, to be your true self.

The filled in Step 5 chart on the following page shares some entries other people have made onto their own charts, including their bigger yeses. Of course, your entries may be quite different.

Step 5
Choosing My Bigger Yes
Exercise Examples

1.
PUSH

When Michael, who I am working on a project with, didn't return my phone call.

LIMITING BELIEF (False I Am)

I am needy.

DESIRE

To discuss the project and move forward.

VALUE (True I Am)

I am a collaborator. I value productivity and movement.

MY BIGGER YES

I realize how much I love collaborating on projects and what a great collaborator I am.

2.
PUSH

Talking to my friend about her retirement plans.

LIMITING BELIEF (False I Am)

I am a failure.

DESIRE

To live my life in the moment. To appreciate each day.

VALUE (True I Am)

I am spontaneous, flexible, and adventurous.

MY BIGGER YES

I admit I love my life.

3.
PUSH

Agreeing to be the treasurer of our club.

LIMITING BELIEF (False I Am)

I am lazy.

DESIRE

I want to spend more time with my family.

VALUE (True I Am)

I am loving and caring.

MY BIGGER YES
I am going to tell members of my club that now is not the right time for me to take on the position of treasurer.

4.
PUSH
Noticing a colleague's hourly rate on his website.
LIMITING BELIEF (False I Am)
I do not value myself.
DESIRE
To share my work with many people.
VALUE (True I Am)
I am valuable and I value the work I am doing and how I do it.
MY BIGGER YES
I will stop comparing myself to others.

5.
PUSH
Not having the money to pay off my credit card bill this month.
LIMITING BELIEF (False I Am)
I am foolish.
DESIRE
To give my parents an anniversary party.
VALUE (True I Am)
I am competent, and I value family connection.
MY BIGGER YES
I will allow myself to enjoy the whole process of my parents' party. And I will set up a schedule to repay the debt I incur.

6.
PUSH
My boss scheduled a late afternoon meeting.
LIMITING BELIEF (False I Am)
I am unimportant.
DESIRE
To prepare dinner for my wife.

VALUE (True I Am)

I am punctual. I am present. I value time with my wife.

MY BIGGER YES

Have a discussion with my boss and tell him I have to leave no later than 5:30 P.M.

7.

PUSH

Hanging up my new clothes.

LIMITING BELIEF (False I Am)

I am irresponsible.

DESIRE

To buy a new dress for the party.

VALUE (True I Am)

I am responsible.

MY BIGGER YES

I trust myself to make wise decisions with money.

*LOOKING DEEPER AND DEEPER …
CHOOSING BIGGER AND BIGGER YESES*

Now that you have completed your own Step 5 chart, take a moment to think about what it means to choose your bigger yes in each of the instances you list on your chart. You may feel that you are dealing with more than the particular issues listed on the Step 5 examples chart on the previous page. This is quite possible. Many bigger yeses are big, very big.

With the bigger yes, you are saying yes to yourself. You are saying yes to how your energy wants to flow. You are also saying yes to something bigger:

**You are aligning
your energy
with
how this energy
naturally wants to flow.**

**You are allowing
your energy to
flow in alignment with
your values.**

**You are living
a life of integrity
and what follows is
an inner peace.**

Since we don't live in a bubble, since we are part of all that is around and within us, how we use and flow our energy matters. You can check this out in your own life. Do you prefer interacting with people that are angry, resentful and bitter – or with people that are joyful, open and inspired? How is the quality of your daily life affected when you interact with these two very different energies?

When you are living authentically and in integrity with yourself, you are sharing the gift that you are here to share. You are not withholding yourself and your energy, trying to pretend you are someone you are not. When you are sharing the gift that you are, you will notice that your life is working better.

And you will find that as you more and more authentically flow your energy, others around you will be inspired by your authenticity.

CHOOSING YOUR BIGGER YES AND FADING OUT LIMITING BELIEFS

This process of looking for and choosing your bigger yeses will naturally help you break free of your limiting beliefs. You will see any limiting beliefs affecting you with greater and greater clarity. These limiting beliefs will begin to loosen their grip on you, to dislodge. Then you will feel safe letting these limiting beliefs go because you realize the power they have had over you is no longer there.

And then you can get back on track, you can live your desires and values and feel the inspiration flowing within you. As soon as this inspiration begins to flow, those limiting beliefs lose their ability to get you off track. Those limiting beliefs no longer have the power to obstruct the flow of your energy.

When we look at other people's examples (of their own letting go of limiting beliefs in order to be themselves), we may find that this can bring up a sense of judgment in us. We can look at this sense of judging others to understand how others might also react to our own choosing the bigger yes processes. For example, we might say:

> Why does someone have to buy a new outfit to feel good about herself? It's what's on the inside that counts.
>
> > *Someone else may want to buy a new outfit for reasons we can never fully know. This is because that person's reasons are not ours. These reasons are hers or his. We can never know what all is involved in this person choosing her or his bigger yes. And this is most likely none of our business.*
>
> Why is someone throwing an anniversary party for her or his parents without the money to pay for it?
>
> > *This may be a special anniversary, and so this person doesn't mind paying for it over time. For this person it may be more*

important to give the party than to be concerned about the extra interest expense caused by borrowing the money.

We can never know what all is involved in another person choosing the bigger yes for her or himself.

Know that your own responses to another person's choices in life may be an indicator of how harshly you judge yourself, and can also reveal the rules you yourself are living within. Quite often we react strongly when it appears that other people are breaking the rules we are abiding by, the rules that are preventing us from living as our own authentic selves. And yet when other people's choices do not appear to us to be breaking our own rules, we usually feel little or no judgment toward those people.

Each person has the right to make her or his own choices without concern for others' opinions. Each person has the right to choose her or his own bigger yes. Each person has her or his own values that want to be expressed, that want to rise above any limiting beliefs.

Move past any limiting beliefs→→ express your own values.

We have no clue as to what is really going on in another person's life. At the same time, no one else has a clue as to what is really going on in our own lives, not on the deepest level.

This is about you and no one else. Notice the times that you choose to continue to allow limiting beliefs to make the decisions in your life. When this is going on, you cannot be fluid and flexible enough to move into the openings that life presents you each and every day.

Yes, there is always an opening, a choice, that will allow your energy to flow, that will get you back to participating in the giving and receiving flow of life. The process of living as your authentic self by choosing your bigger yes is between you and you. Are you going to be participating in the flow of life, sharing the highest and best of who you are, or are you going to be sitting on the sidelines resentful that the world isn't making you happy?

THE HEALTHY HABIT OF CHOOSING YOUR BIGGER YES

Again let me say that this process of living as your authentic self by choosing your bigger yes is not a one time process. You don't simply choose your bigger yes one time and then you are done. You do this over and over again. You may be doing this choosing your bigger yes over and over again with the same issue and push, each time going deeper into it. Or you may wish to work with several different issues and pushes.

You are reclaiming your wholeness and this requires practice. The practice is one of unkinking the hose so you can get back into the giving and receiving flow. You unkink your hose when you make the decision to choose your bigger yes and be your authentic self.

This is not about working harder – and actually this is often about working less. We work very hard to live according to limiting beliefs, to follow the shoulds in our life. When we are allowing ourselves to be who we truly are, we are in the flow of life.

We work way too hard when we are trying to fix what we perceive are our limitations.

This is a process of releasing the false and reclaiming the true. This ongoing exercise of Choosing Your Bigger Yes will support you in developing the habit of living as your authentic self moment by moment.

To help you remember to choose your bigger yes, always make sure you are affirming the truth of who you are. Be sure you are doing this instead of living out the diminishing identity you may have gotten into the habit of living within.

Say yes to your authentic self. When ever you find limiting beliefs creeping in, you can deny them, and thereby choose the bigger yes. You can say things such as:

> No, it is not true that I am needy: I love to collaborate.
>
> No, it is not true that I am a failure: I love my life.
>
> No, it is not true that I am lazy: I make choices that align with my values.
>
> No, it is not true that I do not value myself: I value myself and the work that I do very much.
>
> No, it is not true that I am foolish: I make wise choices.
>
> No, it is not true that I am unimportant: Who I am and what I want matter.
>
> No, it is not true that I am irresponsible: I trust myself to make wise purchases.

It is your job to pull your power back in to yourself, to affirm the truth about yourself, to be your authentic self. No one else can do this for you. You may become frustrated and disappointed that others aren't reflecting back to you the truth of who you are. However, the more time you spend living as your authentic self, the more you will notice people treating you how you deserve to be treated. If you have been living predominantly from your limiting beliefs, these are what you will notice being reflected back to you. Yet the more you live from your true self, the more you will notice other people's behavior toward you shift.

Yes, by aligning with your true self the compromised limiting belief identity is on its way out. Don't allow any limiting beliefs you may have taken on to hijack your knowing yourself, your true self. You may have been gathering evidence to support your limiting beliefs, to convince yourself these thoughts are the truth of who you are. However, if these thoughts diminish you, they cannot be based on the truth of who and what you are. It is now time to stop tallying up your perceived limitations and start measuring for living as your authentic self.

At the end of the day take a few moments to record in your Bigger Yes Journal those times throughout the day when you did choose your bigger yes. You may have done this with your thoughts, your words, or your actions. Make notes about all this. Record this level of detail.

Notice that when you make the choice to align your energy with your authentic self, the quality of your life continues to improve. Gathering evidence to support your true self is a very important part of Step 5.

Through this process you are deepening the faith you have in yourself and in life. You are experiencing for yourself that it is safe and satisfying to live as your authentic self.

This in turn loosens the grip your limiting beliefs have had on you. With this deepening of faith you will trust yourself more and more when making the decision to choose your bigger yes.

You will see that you are starting to gather new evidence, evidence that shows how much better your life works when you live your own values and follow your own desires ... when YOU remember that YOU direct the FLOW of YOUR ENERGY and can CHOOSE YOUR OWN BIGGER YES for yourself.

To help you confirm your authentic self to yourself, try using statements that include the words "I am." Using these "I am" statements will help you remember the truth about who you are. Instead of going into agreement with your limiting beliefs, you can affirm things about yourself such as these:

I am a collaborator.
I am a contributor.
I am responsible.
I am a good person.
I am making good choices.
I am wise.
I am love.
I am successful.
I am valuable.

I am one with the flow of life.

Feeling your authentic self gently guides you back into the flow of life. Instead of your energy being stuck, YOU WILL FEEL YOURSELF flowing into the openings life offers. Once your energy is flowing in the direction you truly want it to flow, you will notice what begins to show up on the physical plane: a direct reflection of your values and desires.

You will learn for yourself that:

it is safe
and satisfying
to live as
your
authentic self.

PART FIVE

25
Your Personal Evolution Through the 5 Steps

Now that you have learned the basics of the *5 Steps to An Authentically Happy Life,* you are ready to see the larger picture. This larger picture is one of ongoing development, ongoing understanding of the importance of recognizing your pushes and your pulls, and of using this information to . . .

claim your bigger yes,
your yes to
your authentic self.

Once you know the basics of this process of living your authentic life, you begin to see that this is definitely an ongoing process. You begin to see that there are always new opportunities to recognize and respond to your pushes and pulls. You can always find more out about your authentic self. There is always more of yourself to reclaim, to know and to share.

Look at the information you have gathered from the step exercise charts, one for each of the five steps (charts you found in each of the Step chapters in Part Four of this book). Now you are ready to put it all together.

As you read over the notes and charts you made to work the first four steps, you will see in Steps 2 and 3 that your pulls are reflecting back to you who you are and how your energy naturally wants to flow. Your pulls confirm the areas of your life where you are already being or are already seeing who you want to be, your authentic self in the flow of your authentic life. When you record your pulls in your journal, you see these in yourself, and just by seeing these in yourself, you are strengthening your knowing of your authentic self.

Your pushes definitely do contain different information. Your pushes reveal where your energy is stuck. Your pushes point to the hidden, blocked, values and desires that want to be expressed by you.

You can gain information about your authentic self from all parts of this process, from your push/pulls, your values, your desires, and your limiting beliefs. These are your pieces and these are unique to you. Each of these pieces guides you back to the same place, to your authentic self who wants to live your authentic life.

So now that you have had a chance to go through all 5 Steps to Choosing Your Bigger Yes, you may want to practice putting your pieces together. This will help you gain a broader perspective on who you are and who you are not.

To do this, take out all the lists and charts you have made for the five steps, which will include the following charts in your Bigger Yes Journal:

Step 1
Seeing My Pushes/Pulls
Exercise

Step2
Revealing My Values
Exercise

Step 3
Recognizing My Desires
Exercise

Step 4
Understanding My Resistance
Exercise

Step 5
Choosing My Bigger Yes
Exercise

Now, let's put it all together. Now you can learn still more about yourself and the situations you are in. You can start to see the whole picture of who you truly are. And you can see how you want to move, to evolve, more and more in the direction of your authentic self and life.

You can see this process diagrammed on the following page where you will find the Personal Evolution Map #1.

In this map, you see the rising experience of following your pulls in the vertical axis. On this pulls axis, you see the path to your authentic self.

On the horizontal axis which heads downward from the upper left to the lower right, you see the descending experience of being pushed, of following your pushes. This pushes axis is the path to your compromised self.

You can move up the vertical pulls axis and stay in this flow. This can be done by stepping out of the downward pushes of the limiting beliefs that take you away from the flow of your pulls, that take you away from your authentic self.

Study this map to come to further understanding….

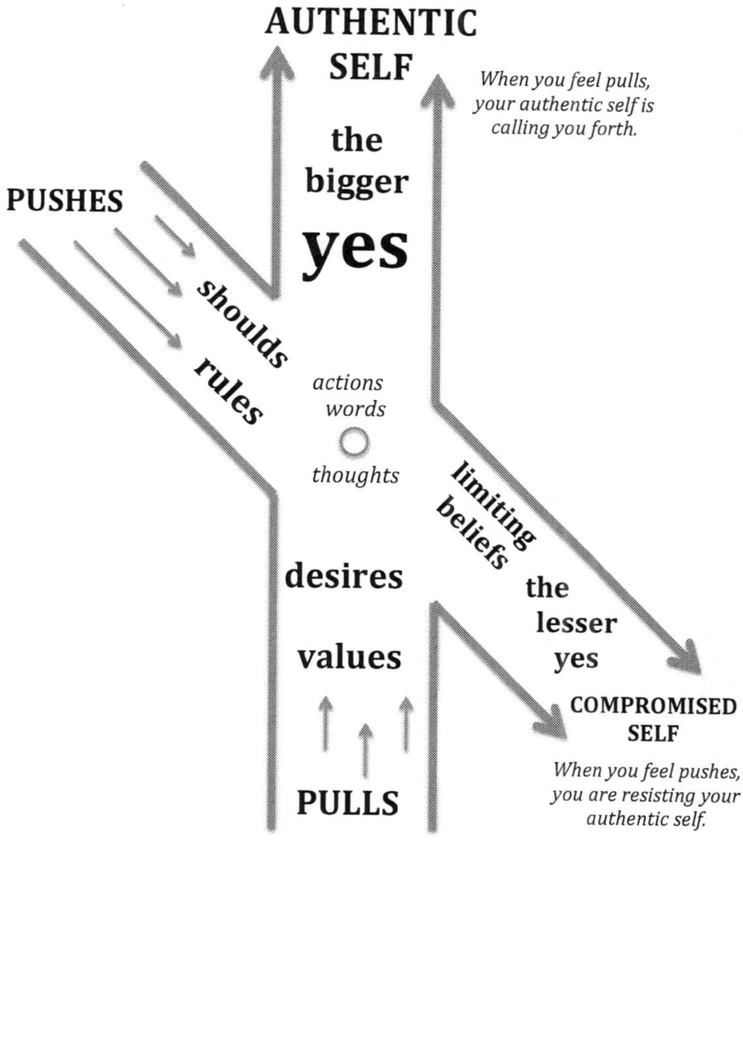

PERSONAL EVOLUTION MAP #1

You may also want to fill in your own map, writing in your own pulls and bigger yeses (with their values and desires) on the upward vertical axis, and writing in your own pushes and lesser yeses (with their shoulds, rules, and limiting beliefs) on the downward horizontal axis.

You can do this using the outline of the Personal Evolution Map #2 here below. Copy this map into your own journal one or more times to work with this….

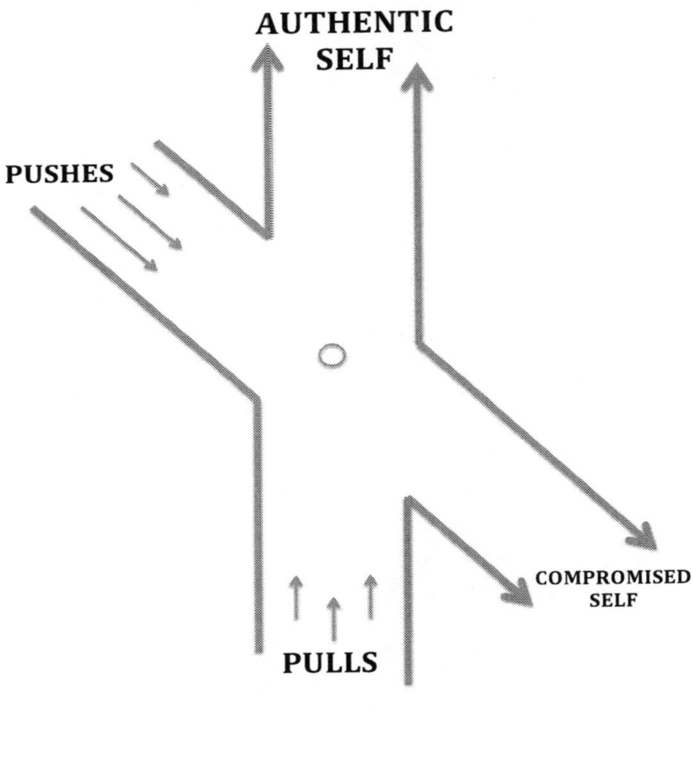

PERSONAL EVOLUTION MAP #2

It is important to know that every time you move beyond a push and go instead with the pull of the bigger yes, you awaken and evolve another part of your authentic self.

The evolution of your authentic self is a very interesting process. When you first begin to work with these *5 Steps to An Authentically Happy Life,* you see that this process is all about you. You are focusing on who you are and who you are not. You are becoming familiar with your values and desires, and with where you get stopped. At times you may even feel you are focusing too much on yourself. However, something wonderful begins to happen when you come to peace with who you are.

You will find that you are no longer preoccupied with defending or trying to prove your worth. As a result, you will have the capacity to expand your focus beyond yourself. Once you are able to relax into who you are, you can see more clearly the behavior of others around you. You can hear with clarity the messages you are receiving from the world, messages about who to be and what to do. You can hear what you have been doing with those messages, what unspoken rules you have been creating for yourself based on those messages (or what you thought those messages were saying to you).

You see that: when you are following the lesser yeses in your life, when you are living out your limiting beliefs, you are compromising yourself. You are listening to, and taking in and internalizing, the shoulds and rules coming at you from outside yourself. You now can see why you may have felt other people were a threat to your authentic happiness.

However, in the process of awakening and evolving your authentic self, you no longer perceive others as the enemy. Even if people are criticizing and diminishing you for not following the limiting beliefs they want to keep pressing on you, you are able to look through the lens of love – and see the understanding, compassion and forgiveness you know to apply. You can now know that everyone is on her or his own journey, and you can trust in that process, and in your own. Now you can see beyond their judgments and criticisms and know the love that lives within all of us.

So, instead of fueling more drama and hurt by confronting the people and what seems to be their judgments about you, you can redirect your energy away from this painful situation. You can remember the truth of who you are. You can remember the truth about them as well: they are on their own paths through their lives. It is not up to you to judge their choices, nor is it their business to judge your choices. As you deepen your faith in your journey, you will notice that you don't react so strongly to other people's passing comments about and criticisms of you.

Once you see this, you can become part of the solution instead of part of the problem. You keep moving into the upward motion of your pulls, living as your authentic self. As your defenses, judgments and fears fade you have more to give others. You know that everyone on this planet wants to be the love that they are. No one really wants to live as her or his pained and limited compromised self.

Ultimately, by setting yourself free you are a catalyst for others' freedom. The evidence of your evolution is reflected back to you in the way you feel. Choosing to stay grounded in your authentic self instead of matching the energy of what you perceive is another's false fearful self allows you to flow the love that you are. This in turn supports others in remembering the love that they are.

We evolve when we choose not to take the bait of our limiting beliefs. And we evolve when we choose not to take the bait of what we perceive are other people's judgments of us (whether these people are judging us, or whether we simply think that they are).

We can evolve together. Our life gets better and so do the lives of the people around us. We become happier, more authentically happy, and so do the people around us.

This process of moving up the vertical axis is something you can do again and again, as life will present you many opportunities to choose your bigger yes. In fact, this process is actually cyclical, as there will always be a new place to work through all this. This cycle is diagrammed in Personal Evolution Map #3.

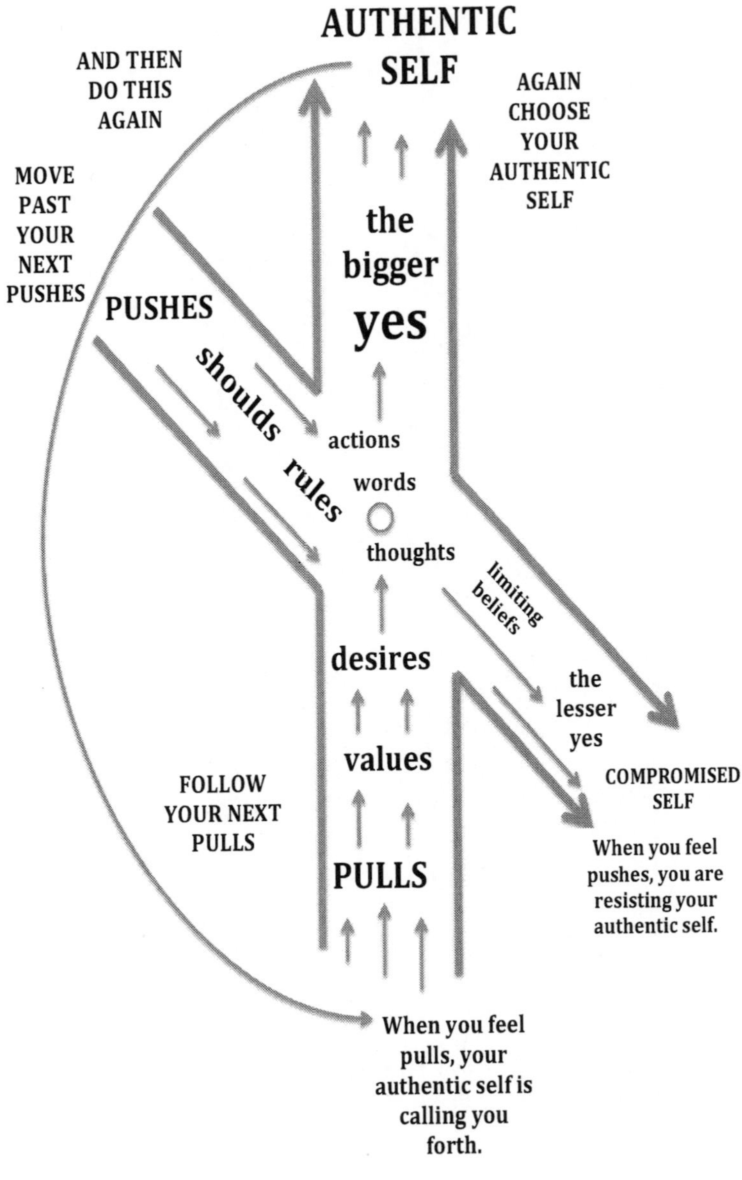

PERSONAL EVOLUTION MAP #3

Now that you have looked over Personal Evolution Map #3, think about repeating this process of choosing your bigger yes again and again, each time with more awareness of what you are doing, and with more understanding of who you are, of your authentic self.

Once you work a while with the *5 Steps to An Authentically Happy Life,* you will find that each time you work through something, you understand more about this process and about yourself. In fact, each time you work through a set of pushes and pulls and then choose your bigger yes, you find you move to a higher level of awareness, a still more authentic self. The energy you find by flowing with yourself, your energy, is there for you to take forward into new areas of your life as the drawing below diagrams.

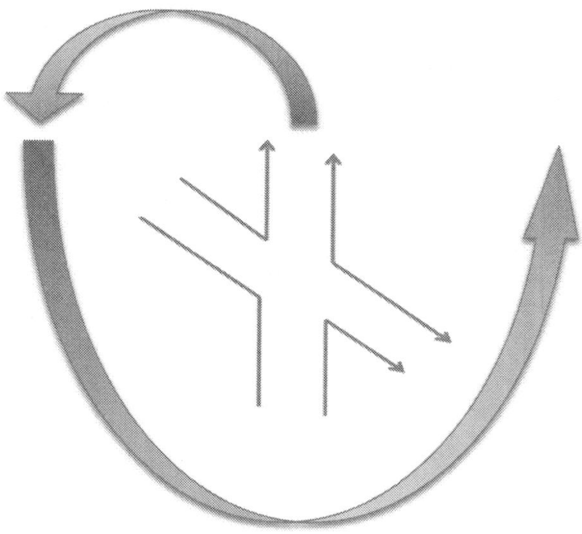

You will see that this cyclic process is actually a spiral. You see that each time you choose the bigger yes, you are moving to a higher level of understanding and your consciousness expands.

As you do this again and again and again – each time you will find a new and higher, more evolved, level of yourself. So this cyclic and rising – spiraling – process is diagramed in the Personal Evolution Map #4 on the following page.

We move past our false, compromised, selves as well as the false selves we perceive others are presenting to us. In other words we take the high road both with ourselves and with others because we know the purity and goodness that people really are.

This is a process that just keeps getting better and better, as the Personal Evolution Map #4 on the following page suggests.

There is no limit to the fulfillment and love that can be expressed through you and as you. You take yourself higher which in turn lifts the energy of the people around you. We are all in this together. Who we are being matters. There is no separation. This is what it is to live fully in the giving and receiving flow of life. Understanding, compassion, and forgiveness keep the energy flowing.

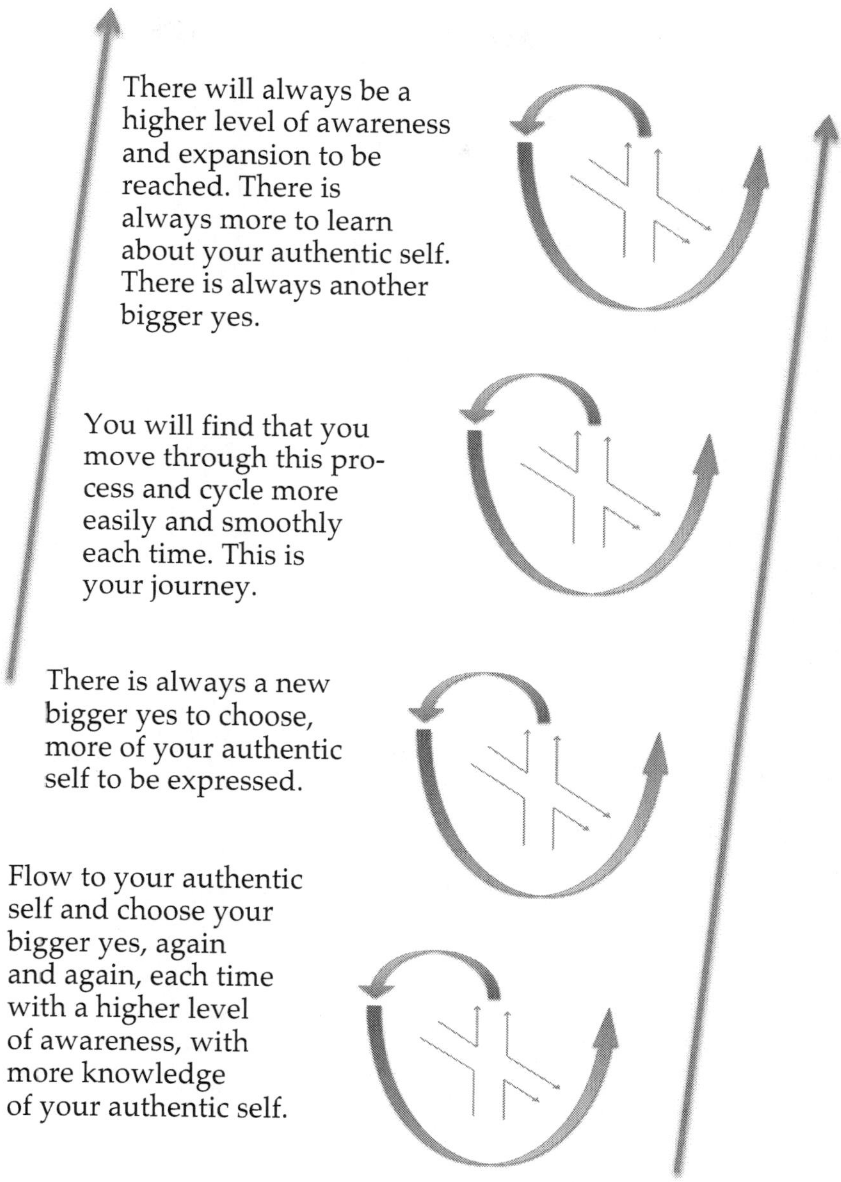

PERSONAL EVOLUTION MAP #4

26
Evolving Moment by Moment

Throughout the day, there are many decisions you are in a position to make. With all the choices you have, how do you know what action to take? When your actions are prompted by your true desires, you are gently guided into the flow. When your actions are trying to fix your perceived limitations, your limiting beliefs, your attention turns away from the flow. Your energy is constricted and you stay stuck – going in circles, repeating the same self-sabotaging patterns of limitation.

Once you are aware that you are in the flow, that you are experiencing a pull, and that you are feeling an inner harmony, you realize you can direct and focus your energy even further. If you have the discipline to align your thoughts, words and actions with your authentic self, instead of allowing them to drift into fear and scarcity, you are in the process of designing your life in a way that reflects your values.

If you are having difficulty deciding whether or not something is a true desire, just follow it. The truth will be revealed. If it is in alignment with your authentic self, the pull will get stronger. And if it is merely there to satisfy your limiting beliefs, your energy around it will dissipate.

If you are listening and discerning between your pushes and your pulls, you will never get that far off from living a happy and authentic life. Strong desires aren't calling you unless they are ripe and ready to be expressed, plucked. If you're not sure if the desire is strong enough for you to pursue at this time, just get closer to it and you'll know. I've noticed that sometimes I'm ahead of myself. Often I'll get glimpses of an idea and want it right now, but when I really check in it's not time for that desire to be expressed. But it is reassuring to know that it is waiting for me to express it when I am ready.

You will come to understand you can trust yourself and what you are feeling. This is a process of getting to know yourself on deeper and deeper levels. You are looking for clarity. And when you have clarity, you will know how your energy wants to flow.

By listening to your desires you are once again guided back into the flow where deep satisfaction and joy are available to you. You can't fully experience the flow when your energy is split.

By focusing on your bigger yes your attention is drawn away from your lesser yes, away from your limiting beliefs.

When your thoughts and desires are going in the same direction, inner conflicts are replaced with inner harmony. Instead of feeling a split in your energy, you feel the oneness with your higher self. The weight of your consciousness is on your values and desires instead of on your limiting beliefs. You can sense an inner momentum of enthusiasm and expectancy building.

Your energy is awaiting your bigger yes to guide you back into the giving and receiving flow. Over time you will learn that you can trust the inspiration you are receiving.

You are not given true desires without having the ability to fulfill those true desires. Listen to your true desires and ask yourself: is this something I can see myself being, doing or having? As long as you don't get sidetracked by your limiting beliefs, you will see that the answer is yes.

It is in our nature to give. Each one of us wants to make the contribution we came here to make – but not as a should, not as an "I *should* care more, help more, do more." Rather, there is an inner longing to experience wholeness and oneness with the world, and to make a unique contribution.

And you are the only person that knows how your energy

wants to be expressed. Therefore it doesn't matter what anyone else's opinion is about what you are doing and how you are choosing to do it. As I explained earlier, this is between you and you. Only you know if you are living life in integrity with your authentic self.

The good news is that every time you drift away from your authentic self, you will be alerted through your pushes.

By following these *5 Steps to An Authentically Happy Life,* you will never get that far away from your center, your authentic self. It doesn't matter how old you are or what you have done in the past. Every moment is a moment you have the opportunity to choose your bigger yes and to get back on track to living a rich and satisfying life. Once you have claimed something of yourself for yourself, the feeling is the same as if you have always had it.

27
Living the Gift That You Are

You may have begun this journey looking for answers to specific problems such as: "I want to know if I should quit my job and, if so, what I should be doing" and "I want to know if I should take that responsibility on, when I don't really want to and don't have the time for it." That people seek answers to questions such as these is not unusual. Many times we find ourselves in uncomfortable, troubled or unhappy situations. When we do, we tend to want to change or fix the situations, to get out of our pain somehow.

Through the steps in this book you may decide to leave your job, or you may find that you love your current job now that you have made the decision to be your authentic self at work. However, the 5 Steps in the book are about something deeper, something bigger than any one daily life question.

By working through these 5 Steps your inner conflicts will be easier to understand and resolve. And there is more: you will feel an inner harmony with your true self. And you will find that something even greater is unfolding.

When you choose your bigger yes you are sharing the gift that you are. The gift that you are is a compilation of your values and desires. You are not fully sharing the gift that you are when you are living as your compromised self. When you are engaged in thoughts such as I am needy, I am a failure, I am lazy, I have no value, I am foolish, I am unimportant, or I am irresponsible, then your giving and receiving flow is constricted and your light is dim.

However, when you make the decision to choose your bigger

yes and admit to yourself that you do love your life, that you do know your priorities, that you do want to be who you truly are, then you can feel yourself back in the flow of your life.

All this is not really about speaking up to your boss, or about deciding whether or not to throw a party, or about making any particular choice in daily life. What all this is actually about is recognizing who you are and acknowledging your own value. What matters is who you are being as you go through life. Are you compromising and shrinking yourself? Are you afraid to be your authentic self?

Or are you embracing the beauty and truth of who you are and the decisions that align with your true self. If you are walking around with the misunderstanding that you are unimportant then you won't trust that you have anything of value to share with others.

Are you going to live the gift that you are? Are you going to follow your true desires? If your limiting beliefs are trying to convince you that it is all or nothing, that you are a success or a failure, a winner or a loser, a good or a bad person, perfect or flawed in some way, well this is not how life flows. Life is not always this extreme. If you listen and look deeply into your pushes and pulls, you will find the harmony and balance that is possible for you. Remember life, your life, is designed to work.

You express your power, your contribution and your love in the world through the sharing of your authentic self. When you are aligned with yourself, when the parts of you are aligned, then you can most surely express your authentic self. Being your authentic self in full is a tremendously fulfilling experience. Your values, desires, and specific abilities seem to take on a magical quality. Yet this is not a magical fantasy, this is really you and really your life. You are living the fullness of the gift that you are.

When you withhold your authentic self, you withhold your gift from yourself and the world. You throw the weight of your consciousness in the direction of your limiting beliefs. Your contribution is restrained, your power is limited, your expression is stifled and blocked. Your joy of being alive is crimped and you are dissatisfied, distressed, unhappy. But of course you are unhappy when you are not expressing your authentic self, as no one enjoys feeling his or her freedom constrict.

No worries though. Just see how easy it is to be in touch with yourself, your true self. You see, your freedom and your happiness are just a thought away. When you are willing to and feel safe to step out and share the gift that you are, there is no limit to the good that can be expressed through you and as you.

When your actions are aligned with your true values and true desires, you can't help but share the gift that you are. It shares itself through you. Your part is to claim your bigger yes by aligning your thoughts, words and actions with what you know to be real and true for you. Fulfillment follows.

WHEN FIRST LEARNING THESE STEPS

When first learning these *5 Steps to An Authentically Happy Life,* these steps can feel a bit mechanical and maybe a little hard to sort out. Was that a push or a pull? Is this mine to do or not? Are these really my values? Can I really tell? Is this a limiting belief I am experiencing, or is this just the way life is?

Questions such as these are right on track and are part of the process of learning to reclaim and then evolve yourself and your life. This is a process of questioning, looking, exploring all you can as you move along the path to greater and greater clarity.

Stay with these 5 Steps and their exercises. Do these again and again. Write down how you are thinking and feeling every day, even many times during each day if you want. You will see how much your clarity increases. This is why your journal can be so helpful during this process. You will want to look back on your journal, your record of the thoughts you have had and the progress you have made.

You can look into your life and see what you are learning. I will use learning to ski as an example here, but know that this process is much the same as the learning of any new skill. At first, trying to ski is awkward and you feel clumsy. It may not even be much fun. While learning to ski, you may get tired of falling down and getting back up.

**Just remember that
falling down
and getting back up
is part of the
learning process.**

At some point, this learning to ski crosses over and becomes fun. And if you keep doing it, it becomes really fun. And before you know it, as you're flying down the mountain, you have no conscious awareness of when you are turning and why. Your subconscious programming kicks in and now you feel at one with the mountain. There is an energy that is pulling you down the mountain and you're just going along for the ride.

This is how these 5 Steps work. As you first move into these 5 Steps, you are very conscious of what you are doing and why. Then, at some point, your muscle memory remembers the truth of who you are and you feel at one with your life. Your primary inner conflicts, those between your authentic self and the compromised self you have been living, dissolve.

Now there is a harmonious flow to your life. Everything is working out for your good and for the good of others. You are happy, fulfilled, your life is working. People around you feel this in you, as you are all beginning to feel the flow together. You see people begin to get in touch with the comfort you have with yourself, your own comfort level, and they want to move in this direction for themselves.

By sharing the gift that you are you inspire others to awaken to the gifts that they are. You also begin to realize that even your pushes can be embraced as opportunities to further evolve.

AS YOU MAKE PROGRESS ON THE PATH TO RECLAIMING AND EVOLVING YOUR LIFE

Once you have travelled awhile along the path to reclaiming and evolving your life, you will reach a point where you actually have to work hard to start messing it up again. Let's go back a moment to the example of learning to ski or learning another skill.

Once your confidence has increased around a particular skill, once you have made this skill your own, it takes a lot of energy to go backward, to return to your old level of this skill, to do this the way you did at the beginning.

Once you become adept at flying down the mountain with skill, you don't go back to the awkward stage of this. You no longer wonder what direction do I point my skiis, how can I keep my skiis together, you just ski. You get into a flow.

This is how it feels when you are in the natural rhythm of receiving your life. Everyday you can enjoy the feeling of flying down the mountain surrounded by beauty and life. Sure some days the weather may be bad, the mountain may be crowded, you may not be feeling so great, but you never question your ability to get down the mountain with grace and ease.

This is the point of sweet surrender, when you stop fighting against yourself. You are in harmony with yourself. Instead of jumping at all the shoulds in your life or berating yourself for not jumping at them, you listen to your authentic self. And you recognize the awakening power within you. You see that this power has energy that wants to be expressed. And you just keep moving into the openings for that expression.

Just like your skiis know where to go, your energy knows where to go too. Now the yeses and noes you say to yourself become quite clear to you. You say yes to your authentic self without a lot of justification and excuses. You cut out the middle man, the noise from the world. You get your inspiration directly from Source, your true self.

Skiing is not fun when you don't have the skills to get down the mountain. The same can be said about life. Life is not fun when you feel confused, frustrated and unable to live your desires. However, as the chaos and drama leave your life, as you reclaim your authentic self, the old chaos and drama is replaced with a sense of self, and of peace and joy.

Now you find a deep knowing and sense of purposeful action. You gain traction in your life like you never before have had. You stop wasting time on what is not yours to do and focus your time and energy on what is really important to you. You begin all this by carving out your reality, making a place for yourself in your consciousness. Then your life begins to reflect your values.

It is this simple: When you are choosing your bigger yes, you are in the flow of life and sharing the gift that you are. You know what the bigger yes means for you because you can feel your energy being pulled. You can feel the difference between choosing your bigger yes and choosing that old lesser yes. You see that when you are settling for the lesser yes, for the shoulds, you are withholding your gift. You also see that when this lesser yes behavior is going on, you feel yourself pushing against or being pushed against. You feel the real difference between your pushes and your pulls. Now you know that it is quite painful not to share the truth of who you are.

So you have realized that when you follow your pulls, your true essence is drawn forth and expressed. You feel the relief of being back in the flow of life.

When you first start working with your push/pulls, this process may feel a little mundane. You may ask things like "How can my reaction to someone cutting me off in traffic have anything to do with living the gift that I am?"

Be patient. As you keep working with your pushes and pulls

and discovering your true values, you will see what is most important to you. You will see that your true desires, which are the expression of your true values, want to be lived through you. You begin to see themes and patterns in your life. You see how even minor things can hold information for you, can help you see who you are and what you are here to do.

28
Evolving Yourself In This World

Choosing your bigger yes is respecting and honoring yourself. This is about awakening to your life, living the life you came here to live, being who you truly are, growing and evolving as you choose to.

A word about the process of using these five steps to awaken and then evolve yourself and your life. Know that the material in this book can be used lightly at first if this feels best to you. You will want to work and rework these steps again and again. Be patient with yourself as you learn more and more about who you truly are and what you truly feel and think.

And be patient with the people around you.

You are giving yourself a great gift. And ultimately you are giving those who know and love you a great gift – and you are giving the world a great gift. However, it may take those around you a little while to see this in full.

So please be patient with the people around you. Have compassion for them as they watch you move through all this. As you embark on this journey, it is not always necessary to announce your process to the people around you.

We often do this when we are unconsciously looking for others' approval, believing we can't move forward with our lives until we gain outside approval. Yet others can't possibly understand what is going on in our consciousness. After all, we're just beginning to make sense of all this ourselves. It would be premature to ask other people to be right there with us as we learn about choosing our own bigger yeses – how to do this and what this means. So, always keep in mind:

this journey is between you and you.

Over the years we have trained the people around us. We have let them see how to respond to us, or at least how to respond to who they and we think we are. People around us come to know how we typically react to situations. They come to know our patterns of behavior. Yet, too often they come to know our compromised selves, not who we truly are. People around us get used to the way we are. When we change, when we evolve, they may react with surprise and pleasure, or they may react with surprise and disappointment.

As you begin to awaken and evolve yourself, you will find that your life, your own thoughts, words, and actions will shift. This shift will be felt by you, yes, and also by those around you. You are part of many people's reality. When you change, their realities change. This can be unsettling for your friends, spouses, children, coworkers, neighbors, and so on.

When your perception of your own self shifts and becomes more authentic for you, be patient with those around you. Know that everyone will make choices to stay the same or to grow at her or his own pace. So, as you evolve using the five steps in this book, others may or may not be right there, instantly shifting with you.

Have compassion for yourself throughout this process of evolving yourself and your life, and also have compassion for the people around you.

29
Yes to Life

Living as your authentic self and evolving your authentic life is about choosing your bigger yes moment by moment. The bigger yes is what your authentic self is saying to you.

If you listen, you can hear your authentic self speaking your bigger yes when you make a choice to or not to think, say, or do something. This is your own bigger yes speaking. You can choose to listen to your own bigger yes, to your authentic self. No one else can choose the bigger yes for you. No one else can listen to your bigger yes for you. So always remember that only you can decide whether to choose your bigger yes.

This is your choice to make.
When you choose to say
yes to your authentic self,
you are affirming yourself
and you are affirming life.

You will become more and more aware of times you are not being your authentic self. Of course, whenever you are not being your authentic self, you are feeling this on some level, in some way. Fortunately, you also know when you are making the decision to be your authentic self.

When you are choosing to be who you truly are, you are in touch with the flow of life – with the love, wisdom and guidance that you can access in this flow every moment.

Once you choose to express your authentic self, you are taking the authentic path. When you lift your head high and make decisions as your authentic self, you can look forward to soaring.

You can look forward to going where you have never gone before, both in your consciousness and in your experiences on the physical plane. You will feel a deeper appreciation for life, not just your life but also all life around you.

The world wants what you have to give, what your authentic self has to share. Otherwise you wouldn't be feeling that spark of true desire within you. Your job and your joy is to trust and follow the inspiration you are receiving.

Your life is not something you have to earn or deserve. Your life is the gift that is yours to receive, and ultimately to give.

There is always enough energy, time, and money to receive your life. This isn't about affording to be authentic. This is about allowing yourself to be authentic. There is no limit to the depth to which you can receive your life and share the gift that you are. So enjoy the journey.

About the Author

Author Janice Campbell began her working career as a CPA and Certified Financial Planner. After many years in the financial industry, Janice recognized that this was not her true calling. Although she enjoyed helping people and working with prosperity principles, there was more she was seeking.

Janice has always felt the presence of God in her life, even as a child. As a young adult, she had been drawn to the writings of the New Thought teachers of the 19th and early 20th centuries. What particularly resonated with Janice was the idea that we are individualized expressions of Spirit and have dominion over our own thoughts, therefore we create our own experiences on the physical plane.

As Janice delved further into spirituality, she found that she loved spiritual teachings. However, she also felt that she needed more concrete information on the matter of living the life she actually came here to live. Janice realized that she was in search of practical steps. She was seeking guidance to help her live an authentic life, a life that reflected her values and deepest desires.

Janice has spent the last twenty years developing and testing her Receive Your Life System. This process can work for everyone, no matter where they are in their lives, and no matter what their belief systems. Janice has distilled her work down to 5 simple steps. These steps are designed to support people in living lives that reflect their true values. Her work makes it easy for people to discover their authentic selves, their true selves.

Janice Campbell is a teacher, writer, and speaker. She lives in Northern California with her husband and children. Janice is a Licensed Unity Teacher and hosts a weekly Receive Your Life radio show.

To order copies of this book, see following page….

To Order Copies of this Book:
This book is available on Amazon, at
www.Amazon.com
You can also locate
order links to this book on this website:
www.ReceiveYourLife.com

To Subscribe to the
Weekly Inspirational Message and
To Join Our Mailing List go to:
www.ReceiveYourLife.com

Author Contact:
janice@receiveyourlife.com

Author Website:
www.ReceiveYourLife.com

Acknowledgements

I wish to thank the many students, clients, and radio guests I have had the privilege of working with through the years. Your presence in my life has been a precious gift. This book is my gift to you in response to all you have shared with me.

I am grateful for the Unity teachings and all the New Thought and other teachers I've encountered along the way. I believe ultimately we are all seeking the same thing, peace in our hearts and peace in the world.

I want to thank Angela Browne-Miller, my brilliant editor, whose contribution extended well beyond the role of editor. I also wish to thank Dennis Owens for his beautiful cover art and his playful spirit.

Last but definitely not least, I want to thank my family, Hugh, Eric, Sean and Christina, the greatest gifts in my life.

Testimonials from Readers, Students and Clients of Janice Campbell

"Janice Campbell is a truly masterful author, teacher, and thinker. Her book, *Choosing Your Bigger Yes*, opened my eyes to all sorts of limiting beliefs running through and affecting my life. I see how all this affects us. The *Receive Your Life System* that Janice has developed is so simple and yet so profound, it is truly life changing."

"Janice is able to cut to the heart of the matter quickly, offering insights and a higher perspective that allow me to reframe the way I'm approaching a challenge. She helps me get in touch with the truth of my Divine nature which opens up new streams of consciousness that lift me out of stuck places. I appreciate her kind, gentle, yet direct and definite approach to working through limiting beliefs that have frustrated and held me back. At the end of a class with Janice there is light, possibility, expansiveness and joy! "

"Janice has a subtle way of nudging you to see the answers you already knew were there."

"Janice Campbell's *Receive Your Life System* has opened me to more of who I really am. I didn't realize the ways I was blocking my own good; I didn't even fully realize that I AM good! I'm happier, I feel free, my marriage is better, and I'm not living out of fear and scarcity. Janice gave direct feedback, got to the point, and gave me tools to use for myself. I was surprised by the quick results, and yet deep and meaningful change."

"Janice's Receive Your Life Teleclass is phenomenal!! The foundation principles/steps are easy to understand and really hit home with me. It doesn't seem to matter what issue or problem each of us on the call might be dealing with, the guidance that Janice provides to one member of the group seems to help all of us apply it to our own situations. Janice is upbeat, compassionate and very encouraging. It's obvious that she 'walks the talk'."

"Janice Campbell is a fabulous teacher! She not only knows her subjects thoroughly, she teaches from what she has experienced herself. Her classes reflect her own deep inner work, her unflagging commitment to truth and her extraordinary ability to guide you to new awareness while always feeling good about yourself in the process. She is, hands down, one of the best teachers I have ever had and my only regret is that I have not been in more of her classes."

Read more about
Author Janice Campbell
and
Choosing Your Bigger Yes

www.ReceiveYourLife.com

4547615R00154

Printed in Great Britain
by Amazon.co.uk, Ltd.,
Marston Gate.